MW00435847

CATHOLIC MANHOOD TODAY

The Handbook

for Building Masculine Virtues and Unleashing your
Strength as a Christian Father, Brother, and Son

By Raylan J. Alleman
© 2015
Preface by Fr. Jeffery Jambon

The creation of man
and woman is the
masterpiece of creation.
[God] did not want
for man to be alone:
he wanted him to be
with his companion,
his companion
on the journey. [1]
- Pope Francis
(Homily February 28, 2014)

[1] Theresa Aletheia Noble, FSP and Donna Giaimo, FSP, Give Us This Day our Daily Love (Boston; Pauline Books & Media, 2015), p 25

TABLE OF CONTENTS

Preface

I truly believe that this book, <u>Catholic Manhood Today</u>, has arrived in a timely fashion. Our society is in desperate need to clarify terms, especially within a Catholic perspective, the non changing realities regarding masculinity. This is most urgently welcomed since the recent tragic mistake of the American Supreme Court's decision on *Obergefell vs. Hodges* which opened the doors to gay marriage at the expense of true holy matrimony. I admire the attempt of Mr Raylan Alleman to persuade us to understand the role of men in a crystal clear way dubbed with great examples. His faith and reason are great assets and are clearly demonstrated here from his perspective "off the bayou" where I too can relate. Mr. Alleman lived for many years along *Bayou Lafourche* and I am from *Bayou Segnet*, so I can attest that his Catholicism runs deep and sincere although both of us are seeing drastic changes around us to the contrary these days. It is precisely this change that we thank Mr. Alleman's bold stance in favor of true manhood and his clever concern to *fix-the-family*. As we are frightened by the massive push for "change" within the "unchangeable", let us remember that the Catholic Church has condemned the frantic efforts of "change of the unchangeable" especially regarding the nature of man and woman. Blessed Pope Pius IX condemned this error in his Syllabus of Errors, originally spoken at an Allocution on June 9, 1862: *"Human reason, with absolutely no regard to God, is the only judge of the true and the false, the good and the evil; it is a law unto itself and is, by its own natural powers, sufficient to provide for the good of individuals and of peoples."* Why is this error condemned by the Church? Because if God is absent from man and his surroundings, then everything is subject to change and since God is timeless, simple, one, His Will is His knowledge, His thoughts are His actions then the consequence is clear - God and His Law is not subject to change. When God says, *Thou shalt not kill,* well that is absolute. It will always be wrong to kill an innocent human being from conception until natural death. When God created made man and woman; male and female - then He creates them thus and he will create them thus until the end of time. So enjoy this delightful, challenging read from an exemplar man, father and friend.

OBERGEFELL ET AL. *v.* HODGES

~Fr. Jeffery Jambon

CHAPTER 1

Catholic Manhood Today

Catholic Manhood Today. Catholic-Manhood-Today. Often we'll hear that there is a crisis in manhood today, that men don't know how to be men anymore. Or we'll hear the question: "Where are all the men?"

Manhood

Let's just say that we as men have our challenges cut out for us. It may seem at times that the deck is stacked against us, that we are constantly under criticism, and that we are mocked as a gender overall in society. Now before you get the idea that the aim of this book is to victimize ourselves as a gender and launch a misogynistic herald against women, it's not that at all. This is just looking at our conditions realistically. The approach here is to look at the way things are, and to be real men and get to work. You'll find throughout this book that we will define and reinforce genuine masculinity for its intended purpose: to defend and protect the weak, to develop society, and to solve its problems.

That's really what manhood is all about. Men solve problems, and let's face it there are many problems to be solved. Again, it's not to cry out in despair and mourn over gloom and doom, or to suggest we're in the worst crisis in history. I just look at it all and say things have been better, and things have been worse. We live in an imperfect world, of course because this is not heaven. Heaven is the perfect world. We are just here for a while. We have a job to do, a role to play, and then we are rewarded for better or for worse on how well we do that job with the cards we're dealt. Each era has its difficulties, and there have been men at the forefront of each society to solve that era's problems. If we look at the great frontiers, discoveries, and inventions they were all made by men. Men just have that vision and tenacity to want to see what makes something tick and to make it better.

Men aren't women. Men are men, and actually God made man first, then woman from him. (cf Gen 2:22) Men are meant to act like men, behave like men. Regardless of any pressures from society otherwise, we need to strive to be real men—tough, strong, decisive, driven. We tend to not be very emotional and possibly not as social, relatively speaking. We don't tend to be overly communicative or very open with our feelings. We are strong, rough, and usually loud. These are natural traits; they are not learned or conditioned. This is the way God made men. If you go to any playground and observe small children playing in a sandbox, you'll typically find the same scenario. The boys will play together separately from the girls with trucks and dozers not speaking to each other but making unintelligible grumbling sound effects that such machinery would typically make. The little girls on the other hand will talk with each other, playing with dolls, having them interact with each other in various role-playing situations. These are the beginnings of manhood, separate and distinct from the feminine.

Manhood Today

Stop and think about what your impression is of manhood today. What do you see? I see basically three types of men: (1) the traditionally masculine man as described above, (2) the man who really never came of age, basically a boy in a man's body, and (3) the feminine man, who may actually have homosexual inclinations. Undoubtedly there have been numerous sociological studies that will aim to discover the reasons for this phenomenon. It's really not my aim here to try to advocate or present those causes. Again, this is where we are, the current state of manhood.

The point of this book will be to emphasize the importance of genuine masculinity and promote it without compromise. God made men and women distinctly different in their anatomy and makeup. "And God created man to his own image: to the image of God he created him: male and female he created them." (Gen 1:27) To attempt to compromise either of the gender's authentic traits would be profane, an insult to God's creation.

Authentic manhood is needed primarily in families for the proper rearing of children. "The conjugal community is established upon the consent of the spouses. Marriage and the family are ordered to the good of the spouses and to the procreation and education of children. The love of the spouses and the begetting of children create among members of the same family personal relationships and primordial responsibilities. A man and a woman united in marriage, together with their children, form a family. This institution is prior to any recognition by public authority, which has an obligation to recognize it. It should be considered the normal reference point by which the different forms of family relationship are to be evaluated. In creating man and woman, God instituted the human family and endowed it with its fundamental constitution. Its members are persons equal in dignity."(Catechism of the Catholic Church (CCC) ¶2201-2203) It should go without saying that clearly it is God's design that families have a father, a man not only involved, but at the head of the home taking responsibility for the lives of his wife and children. Unfortunately, there exists that second group of men mentioned above that behave like a child in the home if they in fact are still present. For a multitude of reasons, they expect their wives to mother them and lead them. This is not God's intent for men in the home. *The principles in this book will reorient men toward their leadership role in the family.*

Authentic manhood is also needed in society at large. Many of society's ills would be fixed by fixing the family. Additionally, men do need to work for the common good, protecting and safeguarding the weak. What would happen if we had effeminate or juvenile men in charge of national defense or police protection? What about firefighting? Road and building construction? These are the roles filled by genuinely masculine men. Obviously many men will also fill roles of more white-collar occupations in society in various professions. They approach their professions in a masculine way with objective technique and decision-making and without undue reliance or interference of emotion or undue concern of offending. Men lacking in maturity tend to blow up in pressure situations and may not be willing to hold a subordinate accountable in order to keep peace, often causing organizations to suffer. Real men do their jobs in a business-like manner and hold to objective standards.

Catholic Manhood Today

Now, to bring this into full perspective: Catholic manhood today. You're probably reading this because you're a Catholic man or you have a Catholic man in your life. Do we ever need Catholic Manhood Today! I'm combining the issues discussed thus far here into the perspective of an authentic Catholic lifestyle. Realistically, Catholic men as a group should be the most authentic manly men. This is not to say there aren't manly men of other faiths. But as a whole consistently throughout, Catholic men should be genuinely masculine. The reason for this is because of the unchanging moral doctrine that guides us. There is no compromise in the Truth. So any attempts to diminish or compromise masculinity should easily be thwarted by Church teaching.

We must have the ability to ward off any pressures to compromise our manhood and any temptations to become lax, indifferent, or frivolous in our responsibilities. To aid us, Christ gave us His Church and the Sacraments. Having recourse to Confession upon events of failure and the sustenance of the literal Body of Christ Himself, we are duly well-equipped for this task. This book integrates Church teaching, practice, and lifestyle with the traits, responsibilities, and roles of true manhood. The complete package is presented here replete with earthy examples and true life stories in simple laymen's terms and backed by the authentic magisterial teaching of the Church.

Finally, there's another aspect of manhood today that I want to emphasize throughout this book. We need manhood _to-day_—now—immediately. The conditions we find ourselves in have put us on a steady decline as a culture. This hasn't happened overnight, and it won't be solved overnight either. But the first step toward recovery has to happen now.

This starts with us, those of us who are men now. If we are insecure in our masculinity, we need to move toward gaining that self-assurance and confidence in ourselves as men. Upon realizing that confidence we need to firm it up in the men around us. Above all, it is imperative that we pass this genuine masculinity on to our sons. They must grow up in an environment with a truly masculine father who demonstrates proper responsible controlled masculinity that upholds family and society. The whole family needs the security that comes from a masculine man, and boys need to see it in action to receive the proper formation of how it is lived in daily life.

Structure of this book

This book is laid out in two principal sections as shown in the table of contents. First we'll unpack our tool chest that we've been given as men containing all the tools we naturally possess as males that just need to be nurtured and developed. These are traits that generally are more pronounced in men and are definitely used in a uniquely masculine approach to interaction with others of both genders. Each chapter in Part I takes one of these traits or tools and thoroughly describes and explains it *in action* with stories and examples. We will explore the unique way God made man with these all important attributes that are so vital to the proper regulation of society. These are definitely traits to be treasured, used, and further developed. Like any other part of the body, if they are not used, they will diminish and weaken. But used properly to their fullest potential, without excess or overuse, will yield the maximum impact for our betterment, and the betterment of our families and society.

Part II of this book explains how we take these tools and use them to mature throughout life as men. All men start out as boys, babies from their mother's womb. We grow and mature and develop, some faster and more completely than others. It is a progression, not an instantaneous transformation. We will go through the progression from being a dependent to becoming independent to becoming interdependent. We will consider the formation of relationships through this process, healthy relationships with both genders of all ages. From those relationships we will proceed into the realization of intimate companionship with a woman that will be permanent through the vows of matrimony. We will then explore the roles in that relationship of a man as leader. That relationship of love will naturally result in the conception and bearing of children, whom the man will also have to lead and father, as only a man can do. Finally we will consider the man guiding his older children into their independence.

So let's get to it. Genuine Catholic manhood awaits. Are you up to the challenge?

CATHOLIC MANHOOD TODAY

PART I – TRAITS – OUR TOOLS

CHAPTER 2

Strength

For God did not give us a spirit of cowardice but rather of power and love and self-control. (2 Tim 1:7)

Strength is raw power manifesting itself in our bodies, our character, and in our duty.

What just came to mind when you read the word strength? Did you picture a large athlete, possibly a football player with bulging muscles? How about a lumberjack chopping down a tree? God has created man in such a way to possess strength. Again, biologically this is more apparent relative to our counterpart of woman. Men are typically stronger than women. Why would God have done this? This is an important question to answer for manhood today because our physical strength is called upon less and less as technology develops.

Did he make us stronger so that we could out-do women, show them up, and make them feel small? Obviously, that's not the case. God made woman after man, to be his help (Gen 2:18). In the reciprocal relationship of love that a man has with his wife, she helps and assists and completes him. He in turn protects, provides for, and defends her. God made her subordinate to him in size and role, but of equal dignity.

With today's technology and our developed society, again these differences between man and woman start to blur. Where is his physical strength needed? Do we need it to provide for her? Again, man once had to go out and slaughter the beast for his family to be fed. But to work today, fewer and fewer men have to use their physical strength in manual labor. I admire a man who does, and enjoy the physical exertion doing outdoor tasks around the house and on our property. It's a very masculine thing to do. I enjoy cutting large tree limbs, of course with a pole-mounted loud chainsaw. I also remember quite a few hot Louisiana summer days over the years at more than one home building fences with my boys. We'd work until I could almost no longer stand. When we use our strength to do constructive things we give glory to God for the men he made us.

But there are other strengths beyond mere physical power. Men possess stamina, courage, and consistency. These are strengths God gives us to fulfill our role as leader of our family and community.

Stamina for work

The most basic demand of our role as husband and father is as provider for our family. God created us so that we would have the ability to do this ourselves. The "help" that our wives give us is to tend to their duties around the home, which they are much more inclined to. When God created for us a helper, it was one who was complementary to us, not the same as us to share our duties. When we are living our roles properly we can each excel at them and be very effective. The problem with so many men today is that they have never heard of being the sole provider or have lost sight of it.

When people ask me what I do, I often tell them I'm a husband and father, if we've never met before. That's my primary role in life. I provide for my family as a certified public accountant, a CPA, or what I often refer to as a "bean-counter." I've been at this occupation for about 23 years now. Like many jobs, it's not one for the faint of heart. We face stringent deadlines and standards enforced by the Internal Revenue Service (IRS), expectations from clients for lowering taxes and timely completion of projects, and pressures from bosses to produce services they can bill out. This can make for some long days (and nights), especially during the first 4 months of the year. But despite these "negatives," I get a lot of satisfaction from rising to the challenges of this occupation, when the skills I have acquired result in a job well done and a satisfied client. This is the way God has created us. Unless we were born into a wealthy family, we have to work for our "daily bread"; it doesn't just arrive at the door. But to meet that need, God blesses us with the strength we need to get it done.

Stamina is strength over the long haul. When we look at the daily grind of the working world, it is very demanding, especially in the capitalist corporate world of today. Regardless, men possess the stamina to thrive in such an environment. We are not meant to be domestic caregivers as women are. Just look at the difference in our anatomy from that of a woman. We are hard and tough; she is soft and tender. She is much better designed for the bearing and caring of children.

In fact, these are the duties God assigned each of us as a result of the fall of our first parents in the Garden of Eden.

> "To the woman also he said: I will multiply thy sorrows, and thy conceptions: in sorrow shalt thou bring forth children, and thou shalt be under

thy husband' s power, and he shall have dominion over thee. And to Adam he said: Because thou hast hearkened to the voice of thy wife, and hast eaten of the tree, whereof I commanded thee that thou shouldst not eat, cursed is the earth in thy work; with labour and toil shalt thou eat thereof all the days of thy life" (Gen 3:16-17)."

As a quick aside, an important thing to note in this Scripture passage that is often overlooked is God's *reason* for his rebuke and punishment of Adam. According to His words, God is rebuking Adam because he *took direction* from his wife, "Because thou hast hearkened to the voice of thy wife..." This is not to say that we must ignore the needs or concerns of our wives. Actually quite the opposite is the case. We need to make decisions based upon her needs and concerns as well as those of our whole family. As fathers, we need to take all into consideration and then make the ultimate decision based on what is best for all considered. That being said, we are not to leave this all important role of ultimate decision-maker to our wives. We do not stand aside as she tells us what to do as though she were our mother. We lead our families and instruct and advise our wives and children of what they are to do.

Woman's redemption would come through her pains in childbirth; man's from his toiling and laboring for his family's nourishment, clothing, and shelter. What an awesome responsibility has been placed upon us by God. We are to do it ourselves while allowing our wives to tend to their responsibility as commanded by God in bearing and caring for children. Unfortunately in our culture today, most men assume their wives will provide an income to the household, and their wives have similar expectations. Even among many Catholics it is seen as mere nostalgia to practice the traditional gender roles in a family of the husband being sole provider and the wife being a stay-at-home mother. But if we are honest with ourselves, we can see how both spouses working outside the home has caused severe weakening and ultimately breakdown in the family. This is not to say that at some times it is necessary or that it is in itself sinful or evil, but it also should not be considered the norm as it so often is today.

We need to take a step back and look at this from a more practical perspective rather than one of an intangible ideal. Based on what we just quoted from scripture, what we men are commanded by God to do is a *job*. Whereas society embellishes it somewhat with a word like "career" as though it is some prize to be sought after. In doing so, women are also lured into "careers" as though it might be more fulfilling than bringing a human being with an immortal soul into the world. Which is more important? Let's take it a step further. Our society is so entrenched in the ideal of dual careers and the exaggerated importance of earning an income that we could be tempted to think that if a mother stays home to care for her children and her husband works that he is in some way superior to her. Actually, I view my wife's role as one superior to mine. To me it's a higher calling to bring human beings into the world and to care for them. Again, viewed more pragmatically, our jobs are actually done at the service of our families. It is in this way that we serve our families. This is not to say that we as men relinquish our leadership but that our leadership is carried out for unselfish purposes.

Sadly so many women are lured into income-producing jobs that take away their dignity and harden them. They try to follow this false construct that women can "have it all" but often end up failing miserably while trying. It is entirely too much of an expectation to put on anyone. We don't have that expectation of men. Why place it on women? Often the result is that a woman will work and then start having children but they interfere with her ability to work. So often after having 2 or 3 children at the most, the couple will either contracept artificially or mutilate their bodies through sterilization. Both of these acts are mortal sins. (see CCC¶2399) Later on after having spent 10-30 years in a job, she is 40-50 years old and quite often regrets missing the greatest mothering opportunities of her life when she was younger but it's too late.

Men, this is our burden to carry. It can be done. We have been blessed with stamina to work steadily and productively for 30-40 or more years. Through our marriages, we receive the grace of the sacrament to also sustain us in the weakness of our flesh. We may need to convince our wives of this way of life as we all have been conditioned with the false ideals of our culture. This is good obedient leadership on our part. Most women with natural mothering instincts will not want to leave a baby at the end of maternity leave to return to work. They should not be forced to do so. Society has trained them to deny these very natural instincts and feelings, and that is a cruel disservice to these women. We have the power of choice to offer our children something better: a mother.

Courage

In what situations in today's world will our courage be called upon? In the developed society in which we live with law enforcement and military defense as well as animal control, we don't face some of the natural dangers men of the past have had to face. In a way, this makes it more difficult to summon our courage at times. When a man has had to face danger and exert courage, he has had valuable experiences that will serve him well. We can see this in those brave men who are in the active military, law enforcement, or firefighting, as some examples.

Courage is not the absence of fear. Courage is the facing and overcoming of fear. This leads us to analyze what exactly fear is. Fear is actually the anticipation of pain. Notice it is not pain itself. So the first thing we need to recognize is that not all things we fear actually occur. According to the website fearofthings.com

- 40% of what you worry about will never happen
- 30% of what you worry about or fear are things that happened in the past and can't be changed
- 10% of what we worry about are considered by most to be insignificant issues
- 12% of what we worry about are issues about our health that will not happen
- This means that 92% of what we fear or worry about will never take place

It should be meaningful to realize that there is only 8% of anything we worry about that can be considered legitimate concerns.

From a spiritual standpoint, the Catechism of the Catholic Church (CCC) tells us "The apprehension of evil causes hatred, aversion, and fear of the impending evil; this movement ends in sadness at some present evil, or in the anger that resists it." (CCC¶1765) I like to state it a bit more plainly: when you sense fear, start looking around for Satan. We really have nothing to fear unless we are not in a state of Grace, if we're in mortal sin. Everything else, we can deal with. Many people fear problems. Don't get me wrong, I don't like problems either. But it helps to know that successful people fix problems. We live in an imperfect world. No one will be without problems. We do our best to prevent problems and avoid bringing them on ourselves, and then resolve that we will handle those challenges that come along in a composed and confident manner.

One of the greatest manifestations of fear that I experience in people is a fear of failure. This fear stops men in their tracks. They are petrified, prevented from doing ANYTHING. Here is another instance where we can look to those who have had success in their endeavors. They realize failing is a possibility, but recognize that failure is an event, not a person or a destination. Until we are dead, we still have the opportunity to recover from failures. We have to realize again, that in the imperfect world in which we live, that things will not always go well or as we intend. If we approach this with the understanding that there is a lesson in every "failure" we can endeavor to take prudent risks in the things God calls us to do. A tremendous help is having someone or several close people around us who believe in us, despite the setbacks we all experience. Ideally, for a man, his greatest fan and supporter will be his wife.

So what would be a practical manifestation of modern-day fears many people have? Probably the most common fear people have is the fear of poverty. In the United States, that's pretty amazing since poverty-level people in our country would be considered to be living as princes in other parts of the world. Still, people worry about money. One thing to be said of this is that it seems to be just as stressful or more stressful to maintain a standard of living as it was to achieve it. So often people will "play it safe" and rarely ever risk anything in what is probably the greatest land of opportunity that ever existed.

My courage was tested when I decided to get into real estate as a sideline venture in addition to my principal job. Actually, looking back the thing that made it most of a challenge was the discouragement that came from people who actually knew next to nothing about it and who would only express their reservations for pursuing it. To overcome the fear, I met with and learned from those who had successful experience in it. They would offer to discuss any questions that I had that would come up. They would listen to my concerns and advise me on how to overcome or address them. Still, there is always that possibility of failure and loss, including until today. There are no guarantees in this life no matter how safe we play it. That has held true for these last 12 years since I first started. Starting took the most courage, but each year gaining experience helps to reduce the fears, like with most things.

Consistency

Consistency allows us to be able to perform day in and day out at a maximum level. Consistency is what I believe to be a man's core strength and character trait necessary to achieve his desired results. We can have all the right intentions and goodwill, but without doing what we have to do, we won't get the results. We can even have all the tools and abilities, but without putting them to use, again the results will be poor. Yet even if we do move beyond mere intention to doing, and even if we put those tools and abilities into motion, but we only apply ourselves part of the time, our results will still be mediocre.

Of course, everyone will have good and bad days, but our very nature distinguished from woman is one of consistency. This is a trait about us that is so needed in leadership positions, especially within a family. A woman's nature is more cyclical. Her body's rhythms send her various phases over the course of each month that affect her physiologically, psychologically, and emotionally. When she conceives a child her body will cycle through a 9-month cycle of changes followed by return to the "normal" set of cycles at some unknown period of time postpartum. Then at a later stage in her life, she runs through a whole separate set of rhythms.

But for us, we're ordinarily the same each and every day all throughout life. This allows us to focus our strength and attention on whatever our endeavors may be. The only thing really stopping us is us, our own will. When we will to do something we can do it, as long as it is within our power. To be successful at anything we have to be consistent with it. The secret of those who are successful is that they do what has to be done even when they don't want to do it. This is so crucial. It holds true in running a business, leading a family, or competing as a professional athlete.

An example of an area I've been able to plainly see consistency and its effects at work is my favorite hobby, running. I've been running since high school—longer than I've been a parent, longer than I've been married to my wife, and longer than I've practiced my profession. I compete at it as well mainly in 5K and 10K road races with an occasional 15K or half-marathon. My sons have also developed into some fine young runners as I've coached them into it, and it's become a great family activity. Running is one sport that must be maintained consistently in order for someone to excel. You can't just run a couple days here and a couple days there. There has to be a set program to follow. It gets to be so necessary that you almost have to plan activities around it. At times I could have a week planned involving 5 training runs, but only was able to get 3 in. If that happens 1 week, it may not show any effect, but let that happen 3 or 4 weeks back to back and you can really see yourself falling back. This is just one example but the same principle holds true for so many things. The most important areas for a married man to watch his consistency is with his relationship with his wife and in the disciplining of his children.

Purity to maintain strength

We'll round out this chapter on strength with a look at a powerful way to maintain overall strength, and that is with the virtue of purity, or chastity. We all have to practice one form of purity or another depending on our state in life in order to remain in a state of grace. We need to be very cautious to guard against sins of impurity because if done with sufficient reflection and full consent of the will they are all considered to be sufficiently grave to constitute mortal sin. "Don't you know that, where purity is concerned, there is no matter that is not considered grave?"[2] This teaching can also regularly be found in good examinations of conscience. It is also worth considering that Our Lady of Fatima warned the children that more souls go to hell over sins of the flesh than any other sin. Does this make these types of sin worse than other mortal sins? Not necessarily, but they are just more common.

This tells me that it takes a great deal of strength to overcome sins and temptations against purity. So in practicing a consistent discipline of chastity by turning our eyes away from pictures or people that could tempt us and by not putting ourselves in situations that could tempt us help to build in us tremendous strength. If we can control our sex drive, we can control any other drive that we possess. There's nothing manly about giving in to the passions of lust. It's actually the stuff of immoral immature boys, even though our society will tell you the opposite. It takes a man of tremendous strength to hold himself in check as he lives in the licentious culture of today.

As with any other behavior, we can train ourselves to reject the temptations to lust. It is necessary to do so as Christ sees lust as one and the same as

---

[2] St. John Bosco <u>Forty Dreams of St. John Bosco</u> (Rockford, IL: TAN Publishers, 1996) p. 34

adultery. (cf Matt 5:28) We should start with avoiding the near occasions of sin so as not to deliberately put ourselves places of temptation like on crowded beaches or in a movie theater playing an illicit movie or aimlessly wandering the internet. But there are some places we cannot avoid like the market or our workplace. Here must be our training ground. As said, we have to form the habit of turning our eyes away from tempting sights. We can easily form the habit of allowing our eyes to wander. It is important to realize we cannot break a habit without *replacing* it with another habit. We have to form the habit of turning our eyes and controlling what we see. But we must also control our thoughts. In the above-mentioned scripture reference, Christ says he who lusts has already committed sin "in his heart." So, we must caution ourselves against even the desire for another and be careful of attractions. Friendships with other women may seem innocent but are the breeding ground for dangerous relationships that often escalate beyond what was initially intended. Our hearts should remain completely for our wives.

The times in our marriages when we have to practice abstinence are ideal intervals when we can strengthen our resolve and form an iron will against the temptations to lust that the devil will want to place before us. At times in the wife's monthly cycle or after she has had a baby or even when you are traveling away separately for work and business can be such occasions. If a couple has to avoid a conception, only natural methods of doing so are permitted for Catholics. Artificial contraception is forbidden under the pain of mortal sin. All allowable natural forms require some form and amount of abstinence. This is healthy good training opportunity for men. Often before we are married we don't realize such instances will occur during marriage. We think that sexual relations will be a constant regular occurrence. If there is one thing we can take from the advent of contraception in marriage is that such constant regularity isn't necessarily the panacea for marriage. Don't get me wrong. I'm not saying marital intimacy is unimportant or can't be a beautiful part of a healthy marriage, but it is just that. It's a beautiful *part* of a healthy marriage and should be the result and expression of an otherwise beautiful marriage. So some times of brief abstinence from marital relations will not be damaging to the relationship but often will enrich it.

For the man who is not yet married and who may be courting, he has to exercise additional cautions. It can actually become seriously sinful for an unmarried couple to deliberately cause sexual arousal by even intimate touching or passionate kissing. If our Lord Himself says that just *looking* lustfully upon a woman rises to the level of adultery, a mortal sin, (cf Matt 5:28), how much more so would deliberately causing sexual arousal in another? They are definitely not permitted to have physical sexual relations of any sort before actually being married. Again, the near occasions of sin must be avoided. For the couple to be alone in secluded areas that could lead to such activity would be a near occasion of sin for most. The man should take the leadership role of strength in not putting himself or his date in the place of temptation.

Purity is an area of strength that is so often undeveloped in men today because they are not required to develop it. Between living in an overall promiscuous society and the false manly stereotype of playing the

Casanova, men are taught to just do as they feel and to give in to their flesh desires. It is a serious weakness to do so. The acts of sexual intimacy are to be reserved exclusively for marriage and to earn this right requires an enduring period of strength and discipline that is the mark of a real man.

CHAPTER 3

Training

Blessed be the LORD, my rock, who trains my hands for battle, my fingers for war. (Psalms 144:1)

Training is the repetition of productive activities toward forming good habits to produce positive results.

Very closely related to and building upon consistency from the strength chapter we have training. Training will build the discipline required to be consistent. While we all do possess strength as part of our character and makeup, we also all are human and get tired. We only have so many minutes in a day; we also will have only so much energy. So we must take advantage of the energy and strength we possess to do productive and important things. The Catholic Faith teaches us that we have an intellect and a will. This is what makes us created in the image and likeness of God as opposed to mere animals. The training of a Catholic stresses the will, more specifically will-power. We are taught to use our will to resist the temptations to sin, to give in to our lower nature. However, we can weaken ourselves and work against our will power by forming bad habits. To overcome them and get back to a productive life of virtue we need to form and keep good habits in their place.

Habits[3]

---

[3] Adapted from The Power Habits System by Noah St. John ©

Who hasn't heard the phrase "we are creatures of habit?" Once we really grasp the truth in that statement we can start to develop some consistencies within ourselves that can yield some magnificent results. This is because we move our actions from a conscious level to our subconscious when we develop a habit, sort of like driving a manual transmission car. Do you remember the first time you tried that? This is not to say that we become robots or zombies. We retain our human dignity while commanding our human nature to do our will.

An important rule of thumb we should use is that is takes roughly 21 days to form a habit. That's a general part of our human nature, our makeup. How often have you tried or heard of someone trying to exercise or diet. They work at it for about a week, possibly 2, and then it gets difficult. The newness and excitement of the new routine wear off. They become weary, and start looking for relief or comfort. They remember how sedation, junk food, or eating to excess provided some pleasure and how easy it was to achieve that pleasure. They also didn't have to even consciously go back to remember how to achieve it, because it was already habitual. So the old habit would just reassert itself. The problem with habits is that the mind does not know if the habit is something good for us or not, it just sends the message to the body to act on the impulse.

We possess the power as humans to command our subconscious and program it into doing what is right and good for us by developing good habits. We simply cannot stop doing bad things that have become habitual.

We instead have to *replace* the bad habit with a good habit. If we know this science, we just need to follow a regimen and work ourselves into a routine of good habits. This invokes the power of momentum. Once we have surpassed the 21-day point, things become much easier in the area we have been working on. This also works from a spiritual standpoint with sins we are trying to overcome. It's not to say that we become perfect, but we have exercised a discipline, some self-denial in order to move ourselves to a higher level, closer to God. This is an extremely virtuous path to take.

Rule

It is very helpful to develop a "rule" of life. This is an idea similar to some of the religious orders, like monks and brothers, but for men who live out in the world, especially in families. I don't necessarily promote becoming part of a secular (or third) order, and I am not in one myself. Instead, I think a man should discern, with the help of spiritual direction, the order that is appropriate for him at his given stage and state of life. If there is one thing I remember from my first spiritual director early on in married life some 18 years ago, it's that we as family men (and those seeking to be) must practice moderation in ALL things, including religion. I've seen so many men who were lax in their faith starting out as a young adult or new parent, and then began having trouble with their families. Then they will "over-correct" and become almost fanatical in their religious practices. This is quite a bit of a turn-off to a wife and children. Instead we need to come up with a regimen of all necessary things that will provide the most productive desired results for those of us who have full lives.

Often, in order to do those things, we have to make room in our schedules. Again, we have to be reasonable and not go off the deep end. Let's look at an example. As a kid, I loved sports, watching them and playing them. While in college, I got away from watching sports on TV as much as I had before. I was a serious student and didn't have time for watching sports. Then once I graduated (Summa cum Laude and third in my class) and moved into the workforce, I found that my coworkers followed sports and talked about it often. So, I got back into it. But I was also married with a child. My wife didn't mind watching sports some, but a kid who is 2 or 3 years old has no interest in it at all. He has his dad home from work and wants some interaction. At the time, the New Orleans Saints weren't doing very well, so watching them caused a bit of an aggravation. All that together made watching football and other sports a dispensable activity to say the least. So, I took the high road and walked away from it again. It wasn't necessarily easy since it had become a habit, but once I had done it, it was nice for everyone in the home. Now most of the kids are older and have an appreciation for athletics and competition and have developed a love for sports, so I'm back into it with them. It's a favorite common family activity for us. But I still find myself having to wander off with our 5-year-old when he loses interest. But can you see how having a "rule" based on our state and life can direct us in activities we should take part in and those we should avoid and how it can change with the stages we go through?

We can take an inventory of how we spend our spare time. We don't have a whole lot of control over our work or sleep requirement, although family men should take family time into consideration when choosing their workplace. But we need to have command and control over our free time. We can purge our schedules of "commitments" to activities that aren't bearing any fruit in our lives. Then we can start to fill them with things that do. What are the ideas that you come across of great things to do "if you only had time?" Write them down, and then make them happen. A good rule of life incorporates activities for financial stability, health, spirituality, good relationships, and service to the Church and community. Find activities that will advance you in these areas and write them down. Begin them, and make them become habit.

Routine and Schedule

Routine is a word that has received a bad rap. It's actually a very powerful tool. It works hand in hand with habits. My family has a routine for days, weeks, months, and years. It's not always so much carved in stone as to not allow for some flexibility as need arises, but it makes it very easy to resume once something has interrupted the routine. The power of routine is that it allows you to do productive effective things without having to think of what to do.

Routine can be worked into a schedule to get that momentum going for good regular repetitions of highly effective tasks. I often use this example when people tell me they don't have time to do things or they can't seem to get to do this thing they've been meaning to do: We're all Catholic right? We're good Catholics.

And good Catholics go to Mass on Sunday right? I'm just wondering how that happens with us being so ridiculously busy. It happens because it's on the schedule. It's set a specific time, and we go at the time it will be done. So setting days and times is key.

Now how do we work around all the non-essentials? Well there's a good analogy you may have seen demonstrated with a jar and some rocks. The demonstrator puts out a jar full of large rocks. It "appears" to be full. He then puts some gravel in, then some sand, and finally some water. What's the point? If the jar was full of water, sand, and gravel, there is no way to get all of the "big rocks" into the jar. Your schedule is the jar. Fill it with big rocks, and you will only be able to allow so much of the sand and water into your life.

Here's an example of our "schedule" as it stands right now for our family Mass and Rosary time.

Day	Rosary Time	Place
Sunday	9:00	In the van on the way to **Mass**
Monday	7:30	At home as a family
Tuesday	5:15	In the van on the way to **Mass**
Wednesday	7:30	At home as a family
Thursday	5:15 7:30	Father and older sons: In the car on the way to **Mass** Mother at home with girls and small children
Friday	7:30	Older kids at Holy Hour Parents with small

		children at home
Saturday	Varies	Depends on if traveling to events

Again, this is a big rock-actually our foundation stone, so everything else stops at these specified times to go to Mass or pray the Rosary. Everything else is worked around it. About the only thing that would be an exception to this is if one of the kids were sick that would prevent them from attending Mass.

This can and should be applied to other areas of our lives. What would be some of the "big rocks" that a Catholic family man should form routines around in addition to Mass and family prayer? Obviously as the provider of his family, his job takes priority. But again, what do we do with our spare time?

One big rock that often is neglected is our health. Just think about how much our health affects everything else in life. When we're younger, it doesn't seem important but as the saying goes, "time flies," and before you know it we're not so young anymore. I was a cross country athlete in college, and I never quit running since. The payoff from this has been absolutely huge. It has promoted the release of stress, clear thinking, proper body weight, and all the health benefits that go along with these conditions. At 45 I still feel very young, have no pain or restrictions at all, sleep well at night, and am at the top of my game in my profession with clear, sharp, and quick thinking. Now I know what you're thinking: that's easy for a college athlete. Admittedly, I do enjoy the activity, but there have been many times (as any athlete or fitness-minded person will tell you) that I would have preferred to stay in bed and miss a run. Of course that has happened many times over the years.

But I have been relatively consistent overall. This is where the power of momentum comes in. Once you can establish a routine and then form the habit, it becomes much easier. I place health early in this list of "big rocks" because of the "domino effect" it has on just about every other part of our lives. St. Paul says to treat the body like a temple (1Cor6:19), and this is why. There are two important elements here: diet and exercise. You don't have to be a distance runner. Some say that running is actually not the best thing for your knees, even though I've been at it 28 years. Walking is excellent exercise as is swimming. Diet is very important as well. We have to eat right; remember gluttony is a capital sin. (CCC ¶1866)

Other "big rocks" for a Catholic family man would be his family's personal finances, including budgeting and investing, spending time with the family, especially our wives, necessary recreation to recharge our batteries, and service to the Church and community. I will elaborate more on many of these key roles later in the book.

CHAPTER 4

Commitment

Commit your work to the LORD, and your plans will be established. (Prov. 16:3)

Commitment is the follow-through in action toward completing the tasks required of your state in life and honoring your word.

True manhood is marked by the ability to make and keep commitments. Of course the most significant of these commitments would be one that would last a lifetime, which would be a man's commitment to his vocation—the priesthood, religious life, or marriage. This very trait is the one that is sorely needed in men today. How often do we hear about men falling down on commitments, being unfaithful to their wives or not doing the thing they said they would do?

At 45 years old, I am a member of Generation X. One of the marks that we are known for is a lack of commitment. Let's look at some of the changes from previous generations where ours may have not been trained in an atmosphere of commitment:

- Mothers began working outside the home more and more not making the commitment to raise their own children.
- Divorce became more prevalent as parents failed in their commitment to each other in marriage to raise their children in a two-parent stable home.

- Priests, nuns, and religious left their orders in record numbers abandoning their vows to God and the Church.
- Employers softened on their commitment to their workers where lay-offs became a common occurrence and pension plans were weakened marking the end of lifetime tenure with a company.

You can probably think of others, but I think these are the most common. Don't get me wrong, I'm not making any excuses for us. But we as a society have to realize we reap what we sow.

Yes, this is the environment I grew up in. I was blessed to have a two-parent home, but I saw my share of lack of commitment all around me. The striking thing to me is the amount of selfishness that drives it all. The next thing I notice is that despite the selfish motives behind the lack of commitment, in the end the uncommitted one is still unhappy. What many fail to comprehend is the difference between misery and temporary discomfort.

Discomfort is a part of life. We are human; we get tired and weak. Donald Trump, well known real estate magnate and entrepreneur, said "your higher self lies outside your comfort zone." This is what Christ calls us to, our higher self. Commitment causes us to keep moving forward in the face of pain or discomfort. Commitment causes us to work through difficulty in our relationships instead of ending them. It causes us to seek to understand our wives and their needs when they get in the way of our desires or selfishness. Commitment causes us to pass on doing things for ourselves to be present to our children and develop a relationship with them so that we can guide them on through life.

In the end, when we lay aside our selfishness out of commitment, we arrive at a place called contentment or joy. I remember Mother Angelica saying on her EWTN live show that happiness and pleasure are things of this world, but joy is heavenly, a spiritual experience. Christ said "Whoever finds his life will lose it, and whoever loses his life for my sake will find it." (Matt 10:39) This is not to say that we are called to be miserable. In another instance he said "I have told you this so that my joy may be in you and your joy may be complete." (John 15:11) We have to be true to ourselves and pursue that which will be truly fulfilling in the unique way God has made each of us. It is a call to maturity, a call away from the childish pursuits of pleasures toward responsible self-giving love. It is a call to make wise choices based on logic and reason and a rejection of making decisions based on emotion and desire.

Commitment takes time; it is not something that comes easy. But it lays the foundation for a solid and firm future. It is like the foundation of a building, of a home. This reminds us of what Christ said about being wise. Those who listened to His words and acted on them are like the wise man who built his house on rock; those who did not act on them were like a fool who built his house on sand.[4] Notice our Lord says the one who ACTS is the one who is wise. It is not sufficient to listen or to learn or to possess knowledge. We must ACT on it if we wish to be wise and not foolish.

---

[4] cf Matt 7:24-27

Commitment requires action. It's easy to talk a good show, but it takes a man to back up his words with action. Little boys tell stories full of fantasy about what they will do. Women pick up on this quickly. A boy tells her what she wants to hear in order to have his way with her. A wise woman will require him to prove himself to be a real man, to make a commitment to her, a lifetime commitment before she makes a commitment to him. The action of commitment doesn't just last for a day or a week or a month. It continues for the required amount of time to meet the task. Sometimes that may be a year, sometimes 10 years, and in marriage, a lifetime.

So, it's important to know what things we should make a commitment to and what things can stay open-ended. This requires us to make priorities in life. For instance, a man should be more committed to his marriage than his job even though his work is a principal part of his vocation as the provider for his family. A man should be more committed to God than to his wife, even though marriage is a Sacrament and the path that will lead a married couple to God in heaven. Let me explain these two examples.

A married man is required to work to provide for his family. When I married my wife, we both had one more semester before we'd graduate from college. The month after we were married, we were blessed to have our first child on the way. We were daring and young and *thrilled* that we "worked." While there was a little bit of nervousness about being parents, we knew we had what it would take since our faith was strong. I remember Missy coming to me when I was in the library preparing résumés to send out for job opportunities (computers weren't as plentiful as they are today). She said "I don't feel too good." I asked, "You think you're pregnant?" She just smiled and nodded. I had 3 job offers before I graduated. I had a decision to make. We had already made the commitment to our child(ren) that she would stay home and mother and raise them. All of the jobs were in the state but 2 of them would take us farther away from family.

As we discerned where we should go, I realized the most important thing wasn't necessarily which job paid the most, but which one would be most conducive to us raising our family. That's the one I chose. My career has continued on with the same priority since. When a job interfered too much with family life, it was time to find a better one. Now I am self-employed and work from an office on the same property as our home so I can be near my wife and children. I still work hard and focus on doing a good job to maximize the income for my family. So, it's not necessarily that money is sacrificed for the good of the family. I actually see it another way. I see that having a sound, well-ordered family life allows me to be a better worker. I've worked with people with family problems. I could tell when they weren't focused on their work. When a worker does a better job, he makes more money, especially if he's self-employed. So, to me it makes sense and has worked out that putting my wife and family first has helped my career.

Next, a man should have a stronger commitment to God than to his wife. I'm sure that example confused some people. But, yes the wife can compete with a man's commitment to God. I'm not so much talking about his pious practices or spirituality, but I guess that is possible. No, this contention will normally surround itself around their sexuality. This is a very dynamic part of the husband and wife relationship. Satan makes this one of his main striking points in trying to destroy marriages. The most common area of conflict tends to be contraception. As the world has so decidedly bought into contraception, even Catholic couples feel it is their right to make the decision to contracept despite the Church declaring it a mortal sin.[5] According to the Guttmacher Institute (guttmacher.org), 98% of Catholic women have used some form of contraception other than natural family planning. This sin does not fall only on the backs of the women. The men in these marriages are also participating in the sin. This is a situation where a man's commitment to his wife is overriding his commitment to God.

It appears those men and women are willing to commit such grave sin as they live in this culture where her fertility is seen as a disease. Since she is the one who would carry the child and put her body at risk and life on the line to give life, those women avoids it at all costs until they are finally willing to take the plunge and then they keeps it to an absolute minimum. We have to realize that this world's philosophy and the indoctrination of it into our women and men are diametrically opposed to the natural law. The Church teaches us that by default a couple should be having babies and only in serious situations should they postpone a conception until the situation passes.

"So the Church, which is on the side of life, teaches that 'it is necessary that

---

[5] CCC ¶1866/Humanae Vitae ¶14

each and every marriage act remain ordered *per se* to the procreation of human life. This particular doctrine, expounded on numerous occasions by the Magisterium, is based on the inseparable connection, established by God, which man on his own initiative may not break, between the unitive significance and the procreative significance which are both inherent to the marriage act.

Called to give life, spouses share in the creative power and fatherhood of God. Married couples should regard it as their proper mission to transmit human life and to educate their children; they should realize that they are thereby cooperating with the love of God the Creator and are, in a certain sense, its interpreters. They will fulfill this duty with a sense of human and Christian responsibility.

A particular aspect of this responsibility concerns the regulation of procreation. For just reasons, spouses may wish to space the births of their children. It is their duty to make certain that their desire is not motivated by selfishness but is in conformity with the generosity appropriate to responsible parenthood." (CCC ¶2366-2368)

The unfortunate and temporary circumstance is to *not* be in a position to conceive a child, not to become pregnant. A pregnancy to a married couple is always a cause for rejoicing and thanksgiving.

> Certainly sons are a gift from the LORD, the fruit of the womb, a reward. Like arrows in the hand of a warrior are the sons born in one's youth. Blessed is the man who has filled his quiver with them. He will never be shamed for he will destroy his foes at the gate. (Ps. 127:3-5)

Our culture has this very foundational matter totally backwards. This is the mark of evil as Satan takes God's creation and twists and inverts it.

A man cannot place his commitment to his wife above his commitment to God for this or any other reason. He cannot be manipulated sexually by his wife. He cannot participate in this sin by having sexual relations that are frustrated by contraception. The sex act is always to be unitive and procreative, that is, out of love and always open to life.

The time to withhold or delay commitment is *before* permanent vows are taken. In terms of courting, engagement, and marriage, a man and woman should take the necessary time during the relationship before making the commitment to objectively evaluate if they are right for each other. This cannot be properly done if the couple is sinfully sexually active. According to Dr. Kim Hardey, a woman is naturally very observant of a man's faults as long as she is in a platonic relationship with him.[6] Once she becomes sexually active with him, she releases hormones that mask his faults, and she remains in a dreamy state about him. We can see why God would arrange things in such a way so that when in a proper state of holy matrimony, she would be less sensitive to his faults and thereby less tempted to be critical of him. But before marriage she should be very sensitive to the complete reality of the man she will enter into a lifetime commitment with. It is helpful to a man to realize this about her and to not draw her to temptation nor allow her to draw him into temptation so they can keep their relationship pure before and into marriage.

Purpose

We should have a purpose to our life, and this purpose should direct us in our commitments and induce us to remain faithful to them. As Catholics, we know from our Baltimore Catechism that our purpose is "to know [God], to love Him, and serve [Him] in this world and to be happy with Him forever in heaven."[7] This starting point of purpose can guide men a very long way. If we have as our primary motive to know, love, and serve God, this will assist us and prompt us to deny ourselves and to follow the will of God in our daily lives.

---

[6] "God's Plan for Sex vs. the Modern View of Sex" audio presentation by Dr. Kim Hardey

[7] Rev. Bennet Kelley, C.P. Saint Joseph Baltimore Catechism, No. 2 (New York, NY: Catholic Book Publishing Co., 1969-1962) page 9

From that directive we should seek to do God's will for us. To know what His will is, we should look to His Church, the Catholic Church. For those of us who are married men, we are to give up our lives (cf Eph 5:25) (our selfishness) and commit ourselves to the needs of our family, first our wife and then the children that come to us. As Catholics we should be the opposite of selfish, that is, generous with regard to our vocation. We should be each deeply in love with our wife and have the solid commitment to her that welcomes the children that come from the love we share. We should not place limits on the generosity of God and the life He longs to send us. Children are a great blessing, a gift, and they continue on what we pass on to them, especially the Catholic Faith.

Having the responsibility of a family, we are driven to provide food, shelter, clothing, and education for them. We find secure employment or start a profitable, reputable business at which we work by the sweat of our brow. (cf Gen 3:29) We work in a spirit of sacrifice in expiation for our sins. A good perspective on how we should approach our work can be found in the Prayer to St. Joseph the Worker composed by St. Pius X:

> O Glorious St. Joseph, model of all those who are devoted to labor, obtain for me the grace to work conscientiously, putting the call of duty above my natural inclinations, to work with gratitude and joy, in a spirit of penance for the remission of my sins, considering it an honor to employ and develop by means of labor the gifts received from God, to work with order, peace,

moderation and patience, without ever shrinking from weariness and difficulties, to work above all with purity of intention and detachment from self, having always death before my eyes and the account that I must render of time lost, of talents wasted, of good omitted, of vain complacency in success, so fatal to the work of God.

All for Jesus, all through Mary, all after thine example, O Patriarch, St. Joseph. Such shall be my watch-word in life and in death.[8]

When we approach our life with a daily duty that we must accomplish out of the commitment to our wife and the purpose of a provider, we are guided to be balanced in our undertakings. With our purpose being to sacrifice for the good our families, we work diligently and drive ourselves toward our greatest potential with a goal toward excellence so that we can provide for our family's needs, a home of comfort and sustenance. We are not lazy, irresponsible, or apprehensive because we know the duty is on us to "bring home the bacon." But this approach also causes us to also balance this duty out so that we are not workaholics and neglectful of our family. The overriding purpose is our commitment to serve God and thereby our family, so we have to work diligently while at work and then leave in good time so

---

[8] The Raccolta by The Rev. Joseph P. Christopher, Ph.D, The Rtt. Tve. Charles E. Spence, M.A. (Oxon.), and The Rt. Rev. John F. Rowan, D.D. Benziger Brothers, Inc. New York, 1957 pp. 366-367

that we can have sufficient time to guide our family and nurture our family relationships. We can see that if purpose is the driving force behind what we do, it will be well-ordered and balanced so that we meet ALL the needs of our family.

Results

The path we lay out for ourselves should be geared toward the *results* we intend to achieve rather than the activities or tasks we'd like to perform. To put it bluntly, in order to get the results we want, we'll have to do the things we don't want to do when we don't want to do them. Fortunately, this comes as no surprise or deviation for a Catholic who is formed in the way of sacrifice and self-denial. Practicing Catholics should realize that sacrifice and self-denial are an integral part of life, but they also actually will yield some very positive results for the things and situations we want.

We can see a plain example of this in the taking care of our body. What is it that our fallen human nature would want to do with regard to diet and activity? We naturally want to eat food that tastes good and lots of it. Often, food that tastes good is not healthy or good for the body and should be avoided or taken in sparingly. Also, regarding activity, we'd like to sleep late and sit around all day at the computer, television, or wrapped up with a good book. But the body needs some physical activity. We have to move around, preferably spending some time at least 3 times a week at elevated activities of exercise. For those who consistently have this lifestyle, the results they have are fewer health problems, a better appearance, more energy, and clearer thinking. They are just as tempted toward sloth as those who do not have this lifestyle, but they do the things they don't want to do in order to achieve the better results.

CHAPTER 5

Focus

Let your eyes look straight ahead and your gaze
be focused forward. (Prov. 4:25)

Focus is the ability to maintain concentration on the task
at hand as well as the long-term plan undertaken.

Another quality that men generally have been granted by God is that of focus. It is said that women can do one thing and have their minds on something completely unrelated. Men tend to be able to "compartmentalize" their lives and activities and this makes for some very productive time in the areas where our time is spent.

We all possess a certain degree of focus, but if it is not cultivated and preserved, it can be diminished, possibly severely. We can nurture our focus by sticking with the activity or task that is currently our duty. Let's face it, as men we wear a lot of hats. Over the course of a day, we can be a husband, a father, a friend, a worker, a boss, a leader, a disciple, and an athlete. You get the picture. By covering so many bases, oftentimes our minds can get pulled into those other things we're involved with rather than the task at hand. The thing to do at these times is to catch ourselves and consciously focus our minds back to what we're doing. It's the old idea "be where you are." "Do what you're doing."

According to Jim Fannin, the most successful of people, athletes, businessmen, executives, investors, etc. have a great sense of focus. In his program The 90-

<u>Second Rule</u>,[9] he trains his audience on how to develop this focus. One particular aspect of it that was a revelation to me was that these superstars have *fewer* thoughts than most people, much fewer. The techniques he teaches in his program equip the audience to reduce the number of thoughts they have in order to develop a sharper focus.

To get completely focused on an activity, we should shut everything else out. This isn't to say that we are unconcerned with our other responsibilities like our families or with our obligation to worship God. It is by diligently and adequately carrying out our life's duties that we fulfill our family responsibilities and give glory to God. I remember a plaque on the wall of the high school field house that said "What I am is God's gift to me. What I make of myself is my gift to God." So, when we're at work for instance, we close the door on our family life, our hobbies, our Church obligations, etc. and we immerse ourselves completely on the task at hand. If there is an emergency that requires our attention, we will be informed about it. We don't have to be constantly on the lookout for something possibly going on. We shut everything out and focus on the task at hand.

It's very much like when we are in Mass, and God wants our complete focus on Him. We shouldn't be fixing the plumbing problem at home in our minds or getting that project out at the office. While at Mass, it should be our refuge, our sanctuary to leave behind that which is temporal and focus on the eternal. It's our time

---

[9] Jim Fanin, <u>The 90-Second Rule</u> (Niles, IL: Nightingale Conant, 2010)

to get centered and to remind ourselves of what is the utmost in importance. Once we do this it helps to prioritize and reorder all the other things we have to do. This is why Mass is so important. It helps us to refocus. We can fool ourselves into thinking that we don't have time or that we can do it ourselves. We think if we can just apply ourselves a bit longer we'll be able to get so much more ahead. But how often have we done that and wasted our time? How often have we stepped away from the grind and went to Mass to be refreshed and recharged and returned to be a much more efficient and productive worker? We can all get wrapped up in what we're doing and neglect our responsibilities. That's not focus; that's indulgence.

Goals

Once we realize that we can sharpen our focus and be very deliberate in our activities, we may come to wonder what activities should occupy this focus. Many people go through life almost aimlessly just doing what everyone else is doing. Are you familiar with the term "herd mentality?" If we follow this, it can make us seem sub-human. Just look around to see if you'd like the results that the vast majority of people are achieving. If so, just do what everyone else is doing. If you'd like to achieve more, you'll have to do things differently. There is a quote attributed to Albert Einstein: "Insanity is doing the same thing over and over again and expecting different results." This applies not only to us doing the same thing repetitively but also repeating things others do. We'll get results similar to those whose activities we imitate.

One of the most powerful tools for achieving more or better is the *goal*. So the first step here is to decide what you want. An example of this came for my wife and me when we started having children. We were introduced to a group of people whose children were different, in a very good way. As we got to know these people more personally, we came to realize that they lived differently from most others and did different things. We liked what we saw, and were willing to do some different things in order to achieve similar results with our children. So, we did, and it turns out we have achieved very similar results to those of these families we had met that are different from the results of the vast majority of people we know.

That example generally illustrates the point of goals, and it is a very important area where we should be very concerned about the results we achieve. Quite often people are very conscientious about worldly and financial concerns, but are haphazard about their family lives. These principles can and should be used for the good of our families. In this way, we can make goals in all parts of our lives that will support the family under our care. So, even if the goals we have are concerning financial and business matters, they ultimately are concerned with our families, or they should be.

Generally goals have to be specific and time-sensitive. So, once we decide what we want, we need to set goals on a timeline and get on the road toward achieving those goals. We should make long-term goals (10+ years), medium-term goals (5-10 years), and short-term goals (1-3 years). I start with the long-term because the place we want to end up long-term will determine what we do in the meantime.

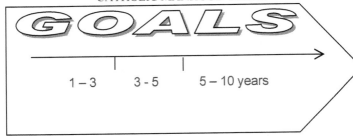

Many do not go through this process because of a lack of certainty about the future. But I believe it's safe to say that everyone has hopes and dreams. This is a good place to start with goal-setting. Check your hopes and dreams, and pursue them with a passion.

I remember wanting to build the office I work from now. I had found a piece of advice that said to get a picture of what you wanted and to look at it every day. Pick a reasonably achievable date to acquire what it is you want. The difficult part (or trick) is to eliminate fearful thoughts. Anytime a negative thought comes to mind, replace it with the picture of the worthwhile goal. So, in the summer of 2009, I set a goal to have my office built by December 31 of that year. This was a very small building that should require about 3 months to build at most. Well, needless to say it didn't go quite that smoothly. There were numerous difficulties and obstacles between permitting, financing, construction, weather, utilities, you name it. But anytime one of these things arose, I returned to that picture and focused on it in my mind. Then I proceeded to the next step in the process without fear. So, on December 31, 2009 I have pictures and video of my sons and me carrying the furniture into my completed office building. Yes, we didn't complete it until the last day, but the goal was accomplished. Since trying that, I have continued to use this execution technique with things that I feel I need to do, and it has served me quite well.

Challenges to Focus

Since we by default will maintain our focus because it is an element of our masculinity, the best way to feed our focus is to avoid those things that obstruct or interfere with our focus. We'll *focus* on those for the rest of this topic.

Distractions

The "developed" culture in which we live is full of distractions. All sorts of media are clamoring for our attention. What once was dominated by the television some few years ago now has been overtaken by personal "devices" (i-phones, smart phones, etc) that travel around with us everywhere we go. It is as though now there is no escape from the commercial media that longs for our attention. This is not to say that these devices are wrong or bad, but quite the opposite. They, as well as computers, can assist us in being efficient so that we can have more time for the more important things. They also are vital in keeping us competitive with meeting the demands of our work life. The important thing is that we use these modern conveniences and not allow them to control us.

If we want to focus on the things that are important, we need to be able to "detach" from these devices and the media. About 12 years ago or so, I started working on personal development very consciously and consistently. It became a passion of mine. I would listen to motivational material almost constantly when I wasn't at work or at home, so that was mostly when driving. As I listened to these business and sales leaders talk about positive thinking and motivation, I would consistently hear them say to shut out the negative. Now this wasn't to say to be totally uninformed, but there is only so much "news" we really need to know. So finally I remember one author on his program say to shut out the news cold turkey and see what happens. His point was that if something was really important, you'd hear about it directly from people. That's the way we're supposed to communicate and socialize. If they don't come out and say, just ask people what's going on. It makes them feel important, and they love to share what they know. Most people love to feel like they are informed and in the know and are quick to let others know about it.

Once I tried this I came to realize that things that once seemed *so* important to me became less and less important. Gradually they started to take on their proper place in my life. One example was sports. I would hear the commentators on talk radio on the morning show go on and on and on about the Saints game all week. During baseball season it would be LSU or the Zephyrs. I was conditioned to think it was just "background noise," but then came to realize it diverted my attention. If I would just turn off the radio I would put very much less thought into those topics. The news was another example. Again, I came to put much less thought into the news pieces. This is one area where technology and the internet can be used for good and becomes a benefit. With the internet you can access all the things you want when you want them. If you need to know the weather forecast, you can get it instantly. You don't have to wait for that segment of the radio or TV news. If you want to know the news, you can determine what news pieces and topics you will consume. My resolution came to be that I was no longer going to turn on the TV or radio so someone else could determine for me what was important.

When we come to this realization, we take a whole new approach to what we will consume with our minds. I have echoes of hearing Zig Ziglar as I listened to him over and over saying "You are what you are because of what has gone into your mind." Our mind is not a landfill for random people to dump their refuse. The problem with so many is that they have come to see the news media as authoritative. What they have to say is of limited use. We have to keep it in that perspective. We need to determine what we take in.

One valuable thing a mentor told me early on was to find the person that has what you want and ask them how they got it. This can save us a lot of time and frustration. How often do we expect someone to teach us something when they have never done it? A teacher is a good example of this. If we want to be wealthy, we can't expect a teacher to teach us how to be wealthy. They may teach us the basic tools we need to function, but unless we apply those tools in a specific way, the results will not be what we intend.

The thing to do is to take a step back and assess what exactly we are taking in, especially on a consistent regular basis. Then we compare that to what we need to be able to accomplish the purpose we identified for ourselves in chapter 4. Is what we are taking in helping or hurting our ability to fulfill that purpose? In this way we can keep ourselves truly balanced. As a Catholic husband and father, I have to be informed about events and politics that affect me and my ability to fulfill that role. I can select to take in those bits of information that pertain to me and the good of society around me.

When we take this step, we can eliminate a great deal of what we take in. This frees up "space" to be able to take in things that are much more beneficial to our vocation.

Programming and indoctrination

What we really need to realize is that these distractions that continue to rob our focus are motivated. They have a very specific motive. They intend to make us do something. The most obvious motive is for us to turn over some of our hard-earned money. Of course it's not stated that way. It's usually stated something like "You've worked hard, so you deserve this....'thus and such.'" Just fill in the blank—new car, hunting rifle, jet ski, etc etc. It's expert marketing coming at you full-speed.

A more subtle motive is indoctrination. Have you ever wondered how on earth we have arrived at such a despicable moral state? Well, obviously moral standards have decreased over time. But if we look around we can see how people gradually start to imitate the things they see on television. This is very crafty work on the part of Hollywood. Now the big rage is tattoos. They seem to be everywhere. Only a very small segment of society had tattoos ten years ago, and now they seem so common. This especially applies to immodest fashion as well, what I call "trashy fashion." Our wives and daughters are encouraged to dress like trash so they can be treated like trash. God had such a greater expectation of decency for females. He warned against men lusting after women in the way they would look at them. "You have heard that it was said, 'You shall not commit adultery.' But I say to you, everyone who looks at a woman with lust has already committed adultery with her in his heart."[10] However, the Church teaches us that women bear responsibility for this sin of lust as much as men do by the way they can draw attention to themselves inciting the passions of men.

> Purity requires modesty, an integral part of temperance. Modesty protects the intimate center of the person. It means refusing to unveil what should remain hidden. It is ordered to chastity to whose sensitivity it bears witness. It guides how one looks at others and behaves toward them in conformity with the dignity of persons and their solidarity. There is a modesty of the feelings as well as of the body. It protests, for example, against the voyeuristic explorations of the human body in certain advertisements, or against the solicitations of certain media that go too far in the exhibition of intimate things. Modesty inspires a way of life which makes it possible to resist the allurements of fashion and the pressures of prevailing ideologies."
> (CCC ¶2521,2523)

---

[10] Matt 5:27-28

Men and boys on the other hand are encouraged to dress in a very sloppy manner. If we look at the effect of these things, it is sloppiness, a lack of discipline, and a push toward relaxation and ultimately laziness. All the while some executive and salesman are getting rich while the masses are getting "everything they want."

As long as appetites for pleasure are being satisfied, the programmers' jobs are done. Studies show that the best way to educate (indoctrinate) someone is to get them in a semi-relaxed state. Have you ever noticed the state you're in when watching television? The actors get you comfortable and they start their indoctrination. Have you ever wondered why they call it a television "program?" They get you in that state and start doing their programming, and it works quite effectively. Our society has to get a grip on its appetite for entertainment and other pleasures if we expect to survive. "Christian purity requires a *purification of the social climate*. It requires of the communications media that their presentations show concern for respect and restraint. Purity of heart brings freedom from widespread eroticism and avoids entertainment inclined to voyeurism and illusion."(CCC ¶2525) "The sensitive appetite leads us to desire pleasant things we do not have, e.g., the desire to eat when we are hungry or to warm ourselves when we are cold. These desires are good in themselves; but often they exceed the limits of reason and drive us to covet unjustly what is not ours and belongs to another or is owed to him."(CCC ¶2535)

To do things well, to strive for excellence, we must have focus. To be able to focus, we have to be able to eliminate distractions.

CHAPTER 6

Standards

*And be not conformed to this world; but be reformed in
the newness of your mind... (Rom 12:2)*

Standards are the boundaries to which we adhere in our
behavior including our dress and language.

The above quote from Romans is one of my
favorite Scripture quotes. We have to have a standard as
Catholic men, and that standard should not vary by the
norms of society. There's another quote I've adopted
that I ran across recently: "I refuse to lower my
standards to accommodate those who refuse to raise
theirs." The world's pull will always be downwards. As
Catholics we know that the 3 main enemies we face are
the world, the flesh, and the Devil.[11]

When it comes to standards, we have to cover
all the bases. We have to realize that the world and
society sees each and every one of us as Catholic. To
our friends and associates, we represent the Catholic
Church. When we behave in such a way in public,
people refer to us as "those Catholics." So we should
present ourselves in a dignified manner wanting to
represent Holy Mother Church well. So this will include
how we behave, how we present ourselves in speech and
dress, how we take care of our health, and what types of
entertainment we frequent. To summarize all of these
areas of our lives, we should carry in ourselves an air of
dignity. This is not the same thing as being snobbish or

---

[11] Cf 1John2:13,15-16

condescending, but one who would garner respect in society.

Masculine Dress

The way in which we are dressed is often our first impression on people, so we have to make our best impact with it. If you just think about it, how do people dress when they are doing something important? I was struck by this in the past few years when the NFL was at a stalemate between the owners and the players. There was news coverage of the players' meetings and court hearings they were attending. Every time they'd show a player, he was in a suit. Why do you think this was? Do you think this is the way he dresses around his home? Is this his most comfortable attire? Of course it isn't. The players' jobs and livelihoods were on the line. They needed to be respected. This was serious business to them. So how did they dress? They dressed in a respectable manner.

On the other hand, how do most people generally dress? They dress as comfortably as possible for the given situation. If we look at that from a Catholic standpoint, this is a form of sloth and giving in to pleasure. Let's look at a man in the home. I remember early on in our marriage when we had just a couple of kids, I would come home and want to get comfortable. So I'd get out of my shirt and tie and go put on some shorts, a tee shirt, and tennis shoes.

Not long after that, we became affiliated with a group of families in which the men dressed a bit differently. Actually, they never wore (or wear) shorts. To them, it was a big deal about how they dressed. They referred to professionals and successful people and how they viewed a man's attire. We've all heard the phrase "dress for success," and we know that doesn't mean to wear what's most comfortable. They would make the point that for even for a man in his home, wearing of shorts would put a man in the same category as a boy. I had to stop and think about that and the way so many men are *treated* by their wives, like little boys. It really all started to make sense. Then I got the revelation that I *never* saw my own father in shorts. Wow! Something clicked for me at that point. Now the only time I wear shorts is for exercise and sleep. I don't hang around my home in shorts. My sons and I are athletes; we run. I formed a running team with them, and we go out and compete in road races. We even have a standard uniform. While competing we wear shorts, but when we arrive and after the race, we are in wind pants, even during the summer. I'm not always in a shirt and tie around the house, but often I am because that is my work attire. But I really believe in men always wearing long pants.

Again, let's take a Catholic approach to this. As Catholics, we look to always do our best; to put our best foot forward. It may be uncomfortable, but that's where overcoming the sin of sloth and offering up our discomfort as mortification in reparation for sin. Works of reparation are actually required forgiveness of sins as part of the Sacrament of Penance, or Confession. "The sacrament of Penance is a whole consisting in three actions of the penitent and the priest's absolution. The penitent's acts are repentance, confession or disclosure of sins to the priest, and the intention to make reparation and do works of reparation."(CCC ¶1491)

Mortification, or denying self of comfort or pleasures, is an excellent work of reparation. "The way of perfection passes by way of the Cross. There is no holiness without renunciation and spiritual battle. Spiritual progress entails the ascesis and mortification that gradually lead to living in the peace and joy of the Beatitudes: 'He who climbs never stops going from beginning to beginning, through beginnings that have no end. He never stops desiring what he already knows. (St. Gregory of Nyssa)'"(CCC ¶2015) So, let's look at the case of a father in the home. Let's say a man is a laborer in his occupation, which is very dignified and masculine. As an aside, I really enjoy manual work. I feel it brings out the masculinity in me in a way nothing else does. When he returns home, he may need to shower and change after a hard day's work. How does he dress then for his evening with the family, in pajamas, shorts, jeans and a t-shirt, shirt and tie? Again, we are standing at the head of the family. We should have plans to have dinner as a family and some prayer time as part of the evening, hopefully a family Rosary. How are we presenting ourselves? I'd say at the least to go above and beyond PJs, shorts, or jeans. How about a pair of khakis and a button-up shirt or polo? None of this has to be expensive or name-brand, just clean and in good repair.

Here's another scenario. How do we dress for Sunday Mass? Now this takes on a vital added dynamic. We're not only "going to Church," but we're going to Holy Mass where we will be in the Presence of our Lord and Savior and Master, Body, Blood, Soul, and Divinity. How do we dress when we're going to see someone important? How would someone dress if he had a job interview with the CEO of a Fortune 500 company?

How would he dress if he were going to see only the President of the United States? How does the man holding that office normally appear when exercising his duties in public? We have to give God our best, and be seen giving God our best, especially by members of our families. For Sunday Mass ideally we should wear a coat and tie, preferably a conservative suit. Again, it doesn't have to be expensive. In our American society, most men do own a suit but only wear it for "special" occasions, like weddings and funerals. Do we see what that might be saying or not saying to our families? Is Holy Mass "special?" The Church teaches us:

> "To prepare for worthy reception of this sacrament, the faithful should observe the fast required in their Church. Bodily demeanor (gestures, clothing) ought to convey the respect, solemnity, and joy of this moment when Christ becomes our guest."(CCC ¶1387)

Again, we are the spiritual heads of our families. We teach in word and action. We lead by example. Our sons when at a tender young age want to emulate us. They want to dress like dad. When they see dad in a suit, they want to wear a suit. I can't express enough how powerful this kind of formation is for our families, especially our sons.

Dignity of a Gentleman

A man's attire is ONLY the beginning of his presentation of himself. Our appearance serves as our first impression, and yes it is only the first impression. This is not to discount that first impression which is why it is covered here first, but we have to move on from that. Before we do, we should consider some modern phenomena that have become quite popular—earrings and tattoos. Neither of these is of an acceptable standard of a Catholic man. Unfortunately, there is a limitation to their removal or reversal. So if a man has taken a step to alter his body in either of these ways, he should do his best to conceal them, especially ridding himself of all ear jewelry. Let's also consider the wearing of hats and caps. Some are necessary for one's occupation or uniform, but should be removed when indoors, less it is part of a required uniform such as in the food service industry. But we see men commonly today indoors with ball caps on and even more inappropriately wearing ball caps and cowboy hats while dining in restaurants! This is not a practice of a Catholic gentleman. It was routinely the practice of a gentleman to remove his hat when entering a building, and Catholic men should practice this to this day.

A man should conduct himself with an air of dignity. Let's proceed here with speech. Profanity should not be a part of his vocabulary. First of all, it is sinful.

> *"Blasphemy* is directly opposed to the second commandment. It consists in uttering against God - inwardly or outwardly - words of hatred, reproach, or defiance; in speaking ill of God; in failing in respect toward him in one's speech; in misusing God's name."(CCC ¶2148)

But from there it is tawdry. As Catholics, we should rise above the culture when it sinks. We should be mature and learned enough to effectively express ourselves without the crutch of profanity. We also need to guard ourselves against excessive use of slang, disrespect, and sarcasm. Of utmost importance is WHAT we actually say more so than how we say it. There are certain types of conversation a Catholic man should be no part of. Gossip is sinful and impermissible as is talk of lewd behavior whether actual or in jest. "No foul language should come out of your mouths, but only such as is good for needed edification, that it may impart grace to those who hear."(Eph 4:29) None of this type of speech has a place with a Catholic man. We represent Christ and His Church everywhere we go and will be held accountable for our actions.

A great deal of focus when we talk about gentlemanly behavior is how a man regards and treats women. It could be said that woman is God's crowning achievement as she was His final creation. Women are the more delicate, more refined gender of human beings generally. They are not to be treated as fellow men, and our behavior should be adjusted accordingly. I really enjoy watching Jane Austen movies, my favorite of which is <u>Pride and Prejudice</u>. My favorite character is Mr. Darcy. I enjoy observing how refined the men were and how classy the ladies were. You can observe how a man would adjust his speech and behavior when a lady was around. It was as if even though he is so refined, he still rights himself further when in the presence of woman.

This whole concept of how we see woman goes much deeper than just our outward behavior around her. How do we view her in our minds and in our hearts? We are all created to be sexual beings, both male and female. Some renounce sexual behavior for the "sake of the kingdom"(Matt 19:12) as Priests or religious but still retaining their sexual nature and subduing it. We all have to practice this discipline to one extent or another as our state in life and circumstances dictate. For even married couples with a healthy sexual relationship St. Paul says will have times of abstinence from relations although they should return together soon so as not to be tempted.(cf 1 Cor 7:5)

Abstinence from sexual activity is a human choice of which we are all capable. It is one of the many ways that our human nature is above that of the animals, a manifestation of an intellect and a will. God created sexual activity as a good to be enjoyed only within the permanent bonds of Holy Matrimony. The <u>Catechism of the Catholic Church</u> states

> "Sexuality affects all aspects of the human person in the unity of his body and soul. It especially concerns affectivity, the capacity to love and to procreate, and in a more general way the aptitude for forming bonds of communion with others."(¶2332)
> "Sexuality is ordered to the conjugal love of man and woman. In marriage the physical intimacy of the spouses becomes a sign and pledge of spiritual communion. Marriage bonds between baptized persons are sanctified by the sacrament. Sexuality, by means of which man and woman give themselves to one another through the acts which are proper and exclusive to spouses, is not something simply biological, but

concerns the innermost being of the human person as such. It is realized in a truly human way only if it is an integral part of the love by which a man and woman commit themselves totally to one another until death."(¶2360-2361)

If we let the words of the Catechism sink in, we'll see that our sexuality is not just a physical reaction but something more imbedded into our being. So it is not something that we share with others like a handshake or a hug. Obviously our culture today has debased itself into relegating sexuality to something almost that liberal. This is simply unacceptable for the Catholic man. He needs to take the lead in moral stature.

For the Catholic man, this means he avoids the "near occasions of sin" as the words of the traditional Act of Contrition put it. We need to have a "custody of the eyes" looking away from women who are not dressed modestly. It takes strength to do this. Men are wired to have their attention drawn to the beauty of a woman's body. Since we are living "after the fall" this attraction can be disordered and drawn to those for whom it is not proper. Some women can dress and behave in certain ways to use their bodies to manipulate or control men. We cannot put ourselves in this position. It is a step toward adultery and our Lord considers it a form of adultery saying "whosoever shall look on a woman to lust after her, hath already committed adultery with her in his heart." (Matt 5:28) Custody of the eyes can be achieved through prayer, penance, and mortification. It is a habit that must be formed. Frequent use of the Sacraments of Confession and reception of Holy Communion keep our spirits strong and able to master the tendencies and weaknesses of the flesh.

A severe dishonor and outright abuse of women is pornography. Viewing pornography is a very dangerous often addictive behavior that causes harm to all involved. The participants who are being exploited in these productions are in no way enjoying themselves. They are victims of all others involved including the viewers. They often have to be drugged to allow themselves to be exploited in the ways they are. The danger to the viewers, mostly men, is that is causes them to view women and sex in a very depraved and animalistic way. Women become objects, or tools, to accomplish a certain end, merely pleasure. It causes them to have unrealistic unreasonable expectations of the intimate relationship they are only to share with their wives and can cause obstacles in intimacy throughout their marriage. This is why the Church warns us so sternly and places such severe prohibitions and punishments against exposure to this moral toxin. <u>According to the Catechism of the Catholic Church</u>:

> "Pornography consists in removing real or simulated sexual acts from the intimacy of the partners, in order to display them deliberately to third parties. It offends against chastity because it perverts the conjugal act, the intimate giving of spouses to each other. It does grave injury to the dignity of its participants (actors, vendors, the public), since each one becomes an object of base pleasure and illicit profit for others.

It immerses all who are involved in the illusion of a fantasy world. It is a grave offense."(¶2354)

So it goes without saying since we are forbidden under the pain of mortal sin, pornography is not to have any part in a Catholic man's life. Anyone who dies in the state of mortal sin will spend eternity in hell.(CCC¶1037) But beyond that factor, we would not want to pollute or compromise ourselves with such vile material. We are to keep ourselves pure. This section is on gentlemanly behavior, and the use of pornography is in no way gentlemanly and will affect our relationships with the women around us. We should not feel surprised or ashamed if we are tempted to make use of it because it is very alluring, disguised as something beautiful and pleasing. It is much like the forbidden fruit in the middle of the Garden of Eden, pleasing to the eye, but deadly to the soul. This is precisely the predictable way Satan operates, very deceptively. This is nothing new. We should not be surprised.

Here is a practical tip: When we are tempted we need to stop ourselves and place ourselves in the presence of God. Slow down the game. Satan wants us to disregard the warning signs and to tell ourselves "we can handle this." We *cannot* handle this. This is nothing to handle. The best thing to do is stop and *slowly* pray 3 Hail Mary prayers. This works wonders at dousing any sparks or kindling that would lead to a ravenous fire of destruction to our souls. Satan *hates* our Lady; he fears Her. She is *always* victorious over him, and it pains him severely to ever be in Her presence or to hear Her name. He flees wherever She is present. Make the commitment to your spouse or future spouse as the case may be to never be duped into this cesspool of foul behavior.

This is in no way any kind of minimum standard that we should aim to achieve in just avoiding pornography. The Catholic man needs to aim to be totally pure. So as a gentleman he will steer clear of all that is vile and decadent. This would go for movies that include nudity or lewd sexual references and profanity as well as indecent conversations and dirty jokes. "Christian purity requires a *purification of the social climate*. It requires of the communications media that their presentations show concern for respect and restraint. Purity of heart brings freedom from widespread eroticism and avoids entertainment inclined to voyeurism and illusion."(CCC¶2525) Our goal is to remain at all times honorable. By removing ourselves from participation in these situations we can silently make a witness to those who may want to involve us. We can influence them to also act honorably. Often we may feel ashamed of wanting to practice virtue, thinking other will think we are weak. This is a trick of the Devil, because when we resist temptation and practice virtue we are being strong. Humans are beings able to be influenced. We never know who we will be able to inspire by acting rightly.

Gentlemanly Standards While Courting

A Catholic man should not begin a committed courting relationship until he can support himself independently and is prepared to support a family. The dating game is not for Catholic men, especially not for Catholic teens. In most cases this would include high school dances and functions that would put teens in the near occasion of sin. The norm is for the girls to dress in provocative revealing dresses and accompany boys (often under the influence of illegal use of alcohol) to a dance where suggestive music is played and the kids participate in lewd dancing. This is not the place for a Catholic gentleman, and not a place for him to bring a young lady. During the teen years, healthy relationships should be developed between boys and girls as sister and brother. It is good for young people to enjoy suitable activities together in groups where there is no pressure to pair up as couples. It is ideal to have adult supervision to accompany them as well. But if the activity is not inherently immoral, kids can enjoy a good time together and start to notice traits and personalities of members of the opposite sex that attract them or repel them. In this pressure-free situation they are able to logically evaluate the type of person they will eventually want to marry as opposed to committed dating relationships that are full of emotion. We will go into relationships more in the "relationships" chapter, but suffice it to say, young people need to avoid the dating scene and take up proper courtship at the appropriate time.

The Upright Attitude of a Gentleman

> *I have told you this so that you might have peace in me. In the world you will have trouble, but take courage, I have conquered the world.*[12]

---

[12] John 16:33

Next in this discussion on gentlemanly dignity, let's look at our general interactions with all of our acquaintances. Catholics generally should be joyful regardless of the trials and challenges of their life at any given time. It takes a strong person to rise above the temptations to be down and still keep a positive outlook on life. This goes hand-in-hand with our Catholic Faith. This is yet another way that we subdue the flesh and keep it under control. We all have different personalities, but each of us can be uplifting in our own way. Instead of focusing on our inconveniences or discomforts at the time, in our interactions with others we should be concerned with how we can be of assistance to those around us. We should always be looking to give, to assist in whatever way we are capable. We all have various abilities that we can lend to the common good of society. We should be generous in sharing the many ways God has gifted us for the benefit of others. Remember God made us strong in order to help those who may be weaker. Relating back to the section on habits, if we are spending our time in this way there is less time we could be involved in sinful behavior. We could be replacing a bad habit with a good one.

Finally on the topic of dignity, we want to present and conduct ourselves in a manner that is respectable. Catholic men should not be a cause of scandal. I recently had a protestant tell me that he was approached on business by a man who represented a Catholic men's organization, and he was obviously intoxicated. What a scandalous representation of our Church! We must realize that we are ALWAYS representing the Catholic Church and should conduct ourselves accordingly. We need to be aware of how we are perceived in public and in our associations. We need to walk and behave with the highest standards. We need to be cautious of the company we keep and the places we go. Some places are just not worthy of our presence. This is not said from an elitist standpoint but from a standpoint of honor and decency, remembering the caution of avoiding near occasions of sin as well as representing the Church well.

CHAPTER 7

Discipline

Those who disregard discipline hate themselves, but those who heed reproof acquire understanding. (Prov. 15:32)

Discipline is doing the thing you have to do or should do even when and if you don't want to do it.

Discipline of course is a very Catholic concept. Actually the root word of discipline is disciple, as in a follower of Christ. A bit of an obsolete definition of disciple is the verb meaning to teach or to train. We can get a lot of practical use out of these meanings. The life of a Catholic is a training in self-discipline. It is discipline or control over oneself and over one's passions and desires. This discipline is exerted on oneself, thus the _self_-discipline. As we mature we should rely less and less on someone else to have to discipline us, but instead we discipline ourselves. The training we receive as children prepares us to be able to exercise this authority over ourselves. We can see then that discipline is an element of and a function of maturity. We can also see how a man who has developed and matured properly is made in the image and likeness of God. The dignity that one who can control himself and his desires possesses is very inspiring and edifying. It is the essence of true strength, true manhood.

Self-denial

Motivator Mike Litman advises that successful people do the things they don't want to do. Zig Ziglar said "When you discipline yourself to do the things you need to do, when you need to do them, the day will come when you can do the things you want to do, when you want to do them." I have come to find out in my experience that applying some of these pieces of advice, normally geared toward business and financial matters, to all parts of life will also yield positive results in those areas. Not only that but it is very much in line with Catholicism. Practicing the Catholic Faith, we will see that Lent always precedes Easter; Advent always precedes Christmas. In each of the examples we see a bit of a give and take, maybe an ebb and flow. Can't we relate to how this is the reality of life? Things are almost never constant. Over the long-term, there will always be change. Also, in each of these examples, some from the secular world, and some from our Faith, we are to give first before we receive. We are to deny ourselves before we replenish. In each case, there is a reward for the sacrifice made. So the thing to remember when we make sacrifices, which is going against our natural desires, is that we are pursuing something, something better, an improvement. In the case of our Faith, we are pursuing heaven. The Church tells us to fix our gaze heavenward.

So we don't experience discomfort because we want to be uncomfortable. If so something would be wrong with us—we'd be a masochist, someone with a mental or emotional problem. We avoid something of lesser value to achieve or acquire something greater. So while it's not pleasurable to deny ourselves, we actually come out better in the end. This is something to keep in mind when we are called to do something we don't particularly want to do or when we feel we want to achieve or acquire something or that we are called to such. The old axiom, "no pain-no gain," comes to mind.

I remember as a kid, being the youngest child in the family, I seemed to always be the last to be able to do something. My brother and sister always seemed to be able and allowed to do things I was not. For the hot summer Louisiana months, we'd go to a public pool for swimming fun and to cool off. Back then in the 70's there were some great diving boards, the ones with a lot of spring in them. (I don't think they are very common anymore with the advent of trial attorneys, but that may have been necessary with the number of critical injuries that were incurred and the amount of danger involved with amateur divers.) Obviously with diving boards, especially the high one, the water depth on that end of the pool had to be pretty significant, 12 feet. So in order to go over to that end of the pool you had to pass a couple of benchmarks. (1) You had to be allowed to enter the pool at all to begin with, and to do that you had to be over 3 feet tall. That took long enough to happen for me. (2) You had to be proficient at basic swimming techniques. To pass this test, you had to be able to swim the WIDTH of the pool (Olympic size) without stopping. Well since I was the baby of the family and always indulged, or so I was told, I was definitely not adept to self-denial or self-discipline or self-control. But I can tell you one thing; I wanted to go off the high dive. When it came time to trying to swim across the pool though, I just couldn't do it. Every time I got about to the middle, I would lose my breath and couldn't go on and someone had to help me because we went to a level of the pool that was too deep to touch bottom without going under water. Then that one time, I'll never forget it, I just decided to PRESS ON even in the face of discomfort, of PAIN. I just bore down and took it. I swam with all my might and breathed and swam and breathed and swam and REACHED the other side, then promptly went on over and took my leaps off those diving boards. That was the first instance I remember of many more occasions which are regular now that I paid the price for something greater that I wanted.

Self-control

> *For you were called for freedom, brothers. But do not use this freedom as an opportunity for the flesh; rather, serve one another through love.* (Gal 5:13)
>
> *Now the works of the flesh are obvious: immorality, impurity, licentiousness, idolatry, sorcery, hatreds, rivalry, jealousy, outbursts of fury, acts of selfishness, dissensions, factions, occasions of envy, drinking bouts, orgies, and the like. I warn you, as I warned you before, that those who do such things will not inherit the kingdom of God. In contrast, the fruit of the Spirit is love, joy, peace, patience, kindness, generosity, faithfulness, gentleness, self-control. Against such there is no law.* (Gal 5:19-23)

I've often told my children that either you'll learn to control yourself or someone will come along to control you. That reminds me of something Jim Rohn once said "Either you have a plan for yourself or you become part of someone else's plan. And guess what they have planned for you: not much!" Well, God has big plans for us, and Satan wishes to hijack those plans and cause them to crash. We have to realize that due to the fall of Adam, we have disordered desires. God makes us with wonderful natural desires, desires for things that are good. But Satan takes them and twists and manipulates them for his own plans. He wants nothing good. He has no power to create, so all he can do is work with God's creation, and he does causing turmoil and anxiety.

Of course God is a God of order and of peace. He created us with the desires of the flesh that we have for good. We are to work and produce and assist others so our bodies need fuel; we need nourishment. So we have the natural desire to eat. It is pleasurable so that we do not neglect the proper nourishment we need. Now we can think of all sorts of deviancies from this natural good can't we? The most common of course would be that with the pleasure of eating, we eat too much. Of course in the Western world, obesity is at an all time high. It is helpful to recognize at this point that gluttony is one of the seven capital sins.(CCC¶1866) Then there is the issue of what we eat. There are so many foods that are unhealthy—junk food, fast food, artificial foodstuffs, and candy loaded with sugar. Of course these are made to be habit-forming and pleasing to the taste so we will buy more and eat more. On the other hand we also have the disorders of those who don't eat enough. This is often the case of the impulsive workaholic who won't stop in order to refuel the body and works his body on fumes.

In the way of nourishment, we should have our three complete meals per day of healthy food that fortifies and strengthens the body. We should not have to have someone forcing us to limit our intake. We should be able to recognize ourselves if we are overdoing it. A good way to bring about this regulation is some regimen of fasting. The Bible encourages fasting when done with the proper disposition.

> *When you fast, do not look gloomy like the hypocrites. They neglect their appearance, so that they may appear to others to be fasting. Amen, I say to you, they have received their reward. But when you fast, anoint your head and wash your face, so that you may not appear to be fasting, except to your Father who is hidden. And your Father who sees what is hidden will repay you. (Matt 6:16-18)*

A good rule of thumb is to work up to being able to have a 24-hour fast once per week. This would of course be for a healthy person. This can start with skipping one meal per week. If junk food is a problem, that could be the first step before skipping any meals—just ridding your diet of junk food. After the body adjusts to skipping one meal, move on to two in one day. I've been doing this for years. The fast goes from supper to supper so I'll never miss all meals in a day, but still accomplish a 24-hour fast.

This same principle can be applied to all of our natural desires. Probably the most common abused desire we have is our sexuality. It is the most difficult to control, so it is the most maligned. This was actually prophesied by Our Lady of Fatima. She said "The sins which cause most souls to go to hell are the sins of the flesh"[13] (meaning sexual sins). (Refer to the previous chapter under Dignity of a Gentleman for dealing with impurity and the temptations related to it.) God gave us the wonderful beautiful act of sexual union for love between married spouses only and for the procreation of children for perpetuation of the human race. It is very powerful, thus the hardest to control. In our current society, this may sound restrictive to be limited to only married spouses. But think of electricity. If not used properly and safely it can be extremely destructive. Married couples share their most intimate beings with each other, and it is in this level of commitment of love that children are to be raised. When sexuality is unrestrained and children are born out of wedlock, they do not receive the upbringing from a loving two-parent home they deserve.

Sleep is another misused desire. Again we can err on both sides with this valuable energizer. The fact that sloth is a capital sin comes to mind here.(CCC¶1866) "Sloth does not catch its prey, but the wealth of the diligent is splendid."(Prov 12:27) Often again since the act of sleeping is pleasurable we are tempted to overindulge in it. How much sleep do we actually

---

[13] Luiz Serio Solimeo, <u>Fatima: A Message More Urgent than Ever</u> (Spring Grove, PA; The American Society for the Defense of Tradition, Family and Property, 2008) p.99

NEED? The typical regimen is 8 hours per night; that should be sufficient. This is a good benchmark.

Of course the other abuse is not enough sleep, usually staying up all night to the detriment of morning responsibilities. This takes a toll on the body after a while. Again, we need balance. It takes self-control to get to bed on time and to rise timely in the morning. As men, we should take this upon ourselves to do without someone having to tell us.

Health

You may have noticed that much of what we've talked about so far in this chapter impacts our health, the health of the body. As Catholics we are to have a high regard for our bodies; it's the only place we have to live. We know that we are body and spirit beings. Our true self is our spirit, or our soul. "In Sacred Scripture the term "soul" often refers to human life or the entire human person." (CCC¶363) Our body is where our soul resides while on earth. Actually the Church identifies death as the point when the soul separates from the body. (So the Church sees the body as something very good, as Scripture tells us.(cf Gen 1:31) According to the Catechism of the Catholic Church

> "The human body shares in the dignity of 'the image of God': it is a human body precisely because it is animated by a spiritual soul, and it is the whole human person that is intended to become, in the body of Christ, a temple of the Spirit: Man, though made of body and soul, is a unity. Through his

very bodily condition he sums up in himself the elements of the material world. Through him they are thus brought to their highest perfection and can raise their voice in praise freely given to the Creator. For this reason man may not despise his bodily life. Rather he is obliged to regard his body as good and to hold it in honor since God has created it and will raise it up on the last day."(¶364)

As Jim Rohn says paraphrasing Scripture, the body is a temple(1 Cor 6:19), not a woodshed. His application there is obvious. As the Catechism says, we are to hold the body in honor. So, we have to take care of ourselves. Above I mention for our health we need the right amount of nourishment and sleep. We also need to exercise our bodies. We have to stay in shape. We know that when we don't move around, when we are too sedentary, our bodies start to tighten up and our muscles and joints don't operate properly and are painful. Throughout history there have been some very holy men who were also very active physically. The patron saint of athletes comes from the early Church, St. Sebastian. "He is patron saint of athletes because of his physical endurance and his energetic way of spreading and defending the Faith."[14] Blessed Pier Giorgio Frassati, a more contemporary figure from the early 1900's, was also very physically active. Of course then there is the recent Pope St. John Paul II who was quite

---

[14] http://www.catholic.org/saints

athletic excelling in football, canoeing, and skiing.[15] These are some models that we can look to in how we handle this part of our lives.

The value to physical exertion can be seen if we approach it from a Catholic perspective. We see all sorts of Biblical analogies that portray active lifestyles in a favorable light. A couple that come to mind are "Do you not know that the runners in the stadium all run in the race, but only one wins the prize? Run so as to win"(1Cor 9:24) and "Whoever wishes to come after me must deny himself, take up his cross, and follow me."(Matt 16:24) The point here is to practice exertion and renounce comfort.

Now this doesn't necessarily mean that everyone has to go out and run a marathon in order to be holy. Personally, I actually don't believe running a marathon is a healthy thing to do for most people, and I happen to be a very avid runner. But I have learned my personal abilities and limitations, and I'm at my best at 6 miles or less and typically won't go further than 10. Regardless, there are all sorts of exercise that can be done. While I prefer running, they say that swimming is the healthiest form of exercise. It is very lenient on the joints, works most of the muscle groups, and is excellent cardiovascular work. However, that exercise necessitates access to a swimming pool. While certain health clubs or YMCA clubs have pools, the inherent downside to them for Catholic men is the near occasion of sin of being around females in bathing attire (or lack thereof). This goes the same for health clubs in general.

---

[15] Rupert Matthews <u>The Popes</u> (NY, NY: Metro Books, 2013) p. 298

So over the years that has reinforced my running regimen and preference. It is easy. All you need is a pair of shoes, and you don't need any equipment or a partner. I have found it to be the lowest cost and most convenient option. However, running may be difficult for some or too hard on the joints. So the most natural exercise for a human being is walking. It has all the advantages of running without the added impact. It's what we were made to do. The health experts recommend 30 minutes 3 times each week. Some form of exercise should be part of everyone's routine who is capable and included in that set of *big rocks* we talked about in Chapter 3 under "Routine and Schedule."

Temperance

If we look for the basic principle in this discussion of this chapter we should come up with the *cardinal virtue* to temperance. According to the Catechism of the Catholic Church,

> Temperance is the moral virtue that moderates the attraction of pleasures and provides balance in the use of created goods. It ensures the will's mastery over instincts and keeps desires within the limits of what is honorable. The temperate person directs the sensitive appetites toward what is good and maintains a healthy discretion: 'Do not follow your inclination and strength, walking according to the desires of your heart' (Sir 5:2; cf. 37:27-31). Temperance is often praised in the Old Testament: 'Do not follow your base

desires, but restrain your appetites' (Sir 18:30). In the New Testament it is called 'moderation' or 'sobriety.' We ought 'to live sober, upright, and godly lives in this world' (Titus 2:12)'(¶1809)

This is a very good explanation with some powerful key words for us to commit to our vocabulary and make a part of our permanent and regular mindset. First let's consider the word "moderates." The term is applied to attraction to created goods. So the things to which we are attracted, and just about all things that exist, are inherently good. We have to recall that Satan cannot create anything so he causes us to sin with the creation of God, created *goods*. So the sin come with excessive use of those goods. We moderate so that we use the goods at appropriate levels. Moderation is such a powerful concept. The phrase "In all things, moderation" comes to mind. Moderation is a strong principle of Catholicism. For instance, many protestants will judge consumption of alcoholic beverages to be evil and sinful even though our Lord made wine for the wedding feast at Cana.(cf John 2:9) In applying moderation, Catholics realize you can enjoy alcoholic beverages without the sin of becoming intoxicated. One must just possess the temperance to limit his consumption before reaching that state. St. Paul warns us that intoxication is a sin "Do not be deceived; neither fornicators nor idolaters nor adulterers nor boy prostitutes nor sodomites nor thieves nor the greedy nor *drunkards* nor slanderers nor robbers will inherit the kingdom of God."(1 Cor 6:9-10)

Let's next consider the term "balance." I remember early on in married life this was the principal concept my spiritual director taught me because this was where I was weakest. I needed to learn to not overdo it in some areas because there was only so much time to go around. It works the same way with goods or pleasures. We have to keep them in proper balance or they can become vices leading to sin.

Finally, let's talk about mastery—what a powerful term. This is how we are made in the image and likeness of God. We are able to master things. With God's grace we are able to master ourselves. When we master something we don't just do, we do it well, as close to perfectly as is possible. We must remember that in order to master something, it takes a lot of training and practice. Professional athletes would be considered masters. They experience a lot of failures even though they are considered the best. While becoming a master they had to go through failure in order to get their craft right. It is the same with us. We can't expect to be perfect right away. We will fail, but we must go to Confession and get back on our way. We have to work hard and diligently at the mastery of these instincts we possess. As we do, we become more dignified and refined as men.

CHAPTER 8

Faith

Trust in the LORD with all your heart, on your own intelligence do not rely; In all your ways be mindful of him, and he will make straight your paths. (Prov. 3:5-6)

Faith the belief in God, a Higher Power, that is always with you and beside you prompting you, assisting you, and guiding your actions.

In this final chapter of the first section of the book we'll consider the concept of Faith. That might seem odd as woven throughout each of the other principles and concepts there has been mention of some dimension of faith. The title of the book tells it's a book about faith, and a particular one in that of the Catholic Faith. But here we want to consider faith first from the standpoint of the real concept of faith as opposed to the practice of the Catholic Faith, or religion, and then as the overriding framework as to how we are to live life.

Faith is a gift

Faith, or belief, is a gift normally presented to us by our parents that we have to accept or reject at some point on our own, be it at Confirmation or at reaching the age of majority or upon leaving the dependency of our parents' home and becoming independent. The Catechism of the Catholic Church states "Faith is a personal adherence of the whole man to God who reveals himself. It involves an assent of the intellect and will to the self-revelation God has made through his deeds and words."(¶176) Yes, faith is a gift that we receive but must nurture and preserve it. "We guard with care the faith that we have received from the Church, for without ceasing, under the action of God's Spirit, this deposit of great price, as if in an excellent vessel, is constantly being renewed and causes the very vessel that contains it to be renewed."(CCC ¶175)

I grew up in the 1970's and 1980's. At that time, faith was still a big part of our culture. Christianity was still quite vibrant and part of the fabric of the Western World. Catholicism was still very strong in my local region of south Louisiana. Much of that has changed. That change started before I was born, from what I understand. In the 1960's some pretty dramatic things happened for the worse.

Personally, I look at this from a standpoint of faith seeing the work of Satan to try to destroy Christendom. We can see his methodical, almost patient work to wear people down over the last century. He has worked to coax people away from good, not under the real appearance of putrid and disgusting evil, but with twisted perversions of the beauty of creation.

So in this contemporary society, we may find ourselves in a minority of believers, those of faith. So, we have to choose if we will actually give our assent to God and accept the faith of whoever presented it to us. We will see as we go through life that there will be many unbelievers: atheists, agnostics, fallen away Catholics, hypocrites, etc. Many people all around us have fallen to the lies of the Evil One. It is not easy to live out our Catholic Faith today. I have felt that from a young age even though individuals and society as a whole were not as hostile to Catholicism and Christianity then as they are now. I believe men of today are better equipped to face this culture than those of my father's generation.

FAITH

They grew up in a very Catholic culture in our region. In other parts of the Western World, the culture was at least Christian. I never experienced that, so I don't have any nostalgic longings for it. As I read the history of the Church, I find that what we experience today is more the norm over the centuries than was the period of Christendom that seems to have lapsed. Has Satan destroyed Christ's Church (the Catholic Church)? He absolutely has not, although some may think so.

Faith requires that each individual make a decision of what he believes and live according to that belief. I have had people challenge my Faith and what I believe attempting to document everything that exists with scientific facts and empirical evidence. My reply to them is that my Faith does not require such documentation. I believe in more than this finite world. I believe in an everlasting life. This world is too imperfect for it to be all that there is. My mother often used to tell us that life is just a test. She was a school teacher par excellence, so this was her analogy of explaining it to us. I learned the Faith from her, so I am well versed in it. So that means there is a definitive "pass or fail" at the end of the test. If you pass you go one way, if you fail you go another. It's just that simple. That also taught me that the test is dependent on what I DO, not just what I think or believe.

"By your stubbornness and impenitent heart, you are storing up wrath for yourself for the day of wrath and revelation of the just judgment of God, who will repay everyone according to his works: eternal life to those who seek glory, honor, and immortality

through perseverance in good works, but
wrath and fury to those who selfishly
disobey the truth and obey
wickedness. (Rom 2:5-8)

Those poor souls who have never been given the gift of faith or who have rejected it live in quiet desperation however happy they may appear to be. The only way to exist under such lack of belief is to live for the natural seeking pleasure, and it will all decay. I believe in a God who has created us for something much better and much greater than that, and I invite you to as well.

Practicing the Faith

Men naturally possess strength and leadership traits to be leaders. We will naturally take on leadership roles wherever we are present. I remember the first couple of jobs I had as a teenager at a small department store and a fast food restaurant. In both of these situations I was singled out for my performance and/or invited into a leadership role in the organization. In the store position I was hired as part of extra seasonal help, and not all of us were going to continue employment after the holiday season was over. A situation occurred where I was chastising a fellow employee for goofing off, and the store manager overheard it. He called me into his office where I apologized. He said "Don't apologize—you'll likely be the one I keep" (employed). And he did. In these situations, I was considered leadership material because I practiced what the organization stood for and followed procedure. It's the seeming paradox that a good follower becomes a good leader.

Similarly, even though we may be leaders we have to submit ourselves to a Higher Authority. First and foremost, we have to live in such a way that is pleasing to God. We have to be obedient to Him. For Catholics, this is very simple since He gave us a Church to guide us until the end of time. All we have to do is to be obedient to the commandments and precepts of the Church, and we can get to heaven.

Confession and Holy Communion

The spiritual life of a Catholic is based in frequenting the Sacraments. We should have a practice regularly going to Confession and receiving Holy Communion. The two go together. We never want to receive Holy Communion unworthily and commit a sacrilege. A practice of regular Confession keeps the soul full of grace by eliminating our sins. A huge dynamic of Confession is its aspect of humility. To go before another man and confess our sins requires great humility. The more we do it, the better we get at it. A good moderate routine for Confession for a layman is weekly or bi-weekly unless of course we have committed any mortal sins, then we should go as soon as possible.

Once we have been cleansed by Confession we are allowed to receive Holy Communion, the Eucharist. I hesitate to say we are "worthy" to receive the Eucharist because who of us could be considered worthy? To stop and consider the Mystery which we will never understand that in the Eucharist we are allowed to consume the Body, Blood, Soul, and Divinity of Jesus Christ our Lord Himself is beyond our comprehension. Of course it goes beyond us being allowed to do so, since our Lord commanded it of us if we wish to attain eternal life. "I am the living bread which came down from heaven. If any man eat of this bread, he shall live forever; and the bread that I will give, is my flesh, for the life of the world."(John 6:51-52) "Then Jesus said to them: Amen, amen I say unto you: Except you eat the flesh of the Son of man, and drink his blood, you shall not have life in you. He that eateth my flesh, and drinketh my blood, hath everlasting life: and I will raise him up in the last day."(John 6:54-55)

My personal experience and understanding is that the Eucharist sustains me and enlivens me as do other Sacraments, but most profoundly. "The Eucharist is 'the source and summit of the Christian life.' 'The other sacraments, and indeed all ecclesiastical ministries and works of the apostolate, are bound up with the Eucharist and are oriented toward it. For in the blessed Eucharist is contained the whole spiritual good of the Church, namely Christ himself, our Pasch.'"(CCC ¶1324) I relate the Eucharist as nourishment to my soul as food is nourishment for my body. It fuels my soul to do good and avoid evil.

As Catholics, we and those belonging to Eastern Orthodox Churches are the only Christians who are allowed to partake of the Eucharist. This gives meaning to the term "Communion" since we must be in communion with the Church to receive the Eucharist. There are many misunderstandings and erroneous beliefs about the Eucharist that abound today. Among protestants I have noticed more than a few times of people saying they believe the "communion" they receive in a protestant service to be the Real Presence. Obviously this cannot be the case as their "preachers" do not possess the capacity to effect transubstantiation. Apart from the Eastern Orthodox Churches, only a Catholic Priest can change the bread and wine into Christ's Body and Blood as his hands were consecrated by a Bishop who can trace his Office back to that of the original Apostles. Conversely and unfortunately many Catholics have lost their faith in the Real Presence of our Lord in the Eucharist. Due to poor teaching and lack of reverence in the Presence of our Lord, many are led to believe that the Eucharist is merely symbolic as it is for protestants. Our belief in the Real Presence must be protected and fortified as our faith is. We will consider later in this chapter ways to do just that in the section labeled "Conduct in Church."

Marriage

Another Sacrament that we "frequent" in a bit of a different way is marriage. Surely we only get married once (or supposedly) as long as both spouses live, but our daily commitment to our marriage is a continual source of grace to nourish our souls as well. This could be said as well for the Sacrament of Holy Orders for a Priest. Catholics view marriage in a very different way from others in society. Many pagans and secularists in our society are seeking to actually redefine the meaning of marriage. Catholics view marriage as a life-long covenant between the couple and God. Christ raised marriage to the level of a Sacrament. It is pure and holy, very intimate and personal between the spouses. It is not something to desecrate and move into and out of so carelessly. By honoring our commitment to our marriages, it not only continues to sustain and inflame our souls, it provides stability to our families giving peace to our children living in a loving home as well as strengthens our society with the firmness of commitment and civility.

The unique and complete relationship of love between husband and wife manifests itself in the intimate physical union of sexual intercourse. This marital union is seen as a very deep and profound good by the Church as long as it is conducted properly, between husband and wife and always open to the generation of new life.

> "Sexuality is ordered to the conjugal love of man and woman. In marriage the physical intimacy of the spouses becomes a sign and pledge of spiritual communion. Marriage bonds between baptized persons are sanctified by the sacrament. Sexuality, by means of which man and woman give themselves to one another through the acts which are proper and exclusive to spouses, is not something simply biological, but concerns the innermost being of the human person as such. It is realized in a truly human way only if it is an integral part of the love by which a man and woman commit themselves totally to one another until death. The acts in marriage by which the intimate and chaste union of the spouses takes place are noble and honorable; the truly human performance of these acts fosters the self-giving they signify and enriches the spouses in joy

and gratitude. Sexuality is a source of joy and pleasure."(CCC¶2360-2362)

Because again we are dealing with a Sacrament, the all important element of grace is effected. "The physical union of spouses is, therefore, sanctified by the sacrament of Matrimony; it is turned into a channel of divine grace...Provided sexual intercourse is carried out properly, it is, again, an effective channel of grace."[16] So when a man is physically intimate with his wife, both receive graces from the Sacrament. This is yet another very beneficial and joyful way of receiving God's Grace to enliven and sustain our souls to do good and avoid evil. We should make every effort to frequent this Sacrament for those men in the married state.

All Catholics need to have a prayer life. Some people will naturally be more spiritual than others, so this will vary among men. Women tend to be more spiritual than men, so they will tend to pray more. Men may be more structured and rote and less "emotional" in the way we pray. Our prayer life will also vary depending on our state in life. A single man, whether or not he is a Priest or brother, will have more time available for prayer than a married man. Regardless, we have to have a prayer life. God wants to hear from us. Our Lord said, "And I say to you, Ask, and it shall be given you: seek, and you shall find: knock, and it shall be opened to you. For every one that asketh, receiveth; and he that seeketh, findeth; and to him that knocketh, it shall be opened. And which of you, if he ask his father bread, will he give him a stone? or a fish, will he for a

---

[16] Javier Abad and Eugenio Fenoy, Marriage-A Path to Sanctity (Manila, Philippines Sinag-tala Publishers, Inc., Oct 1988) p.31

fish give him a serpent? Or if he shall ask an egg, will he reach him a scorpion? If you then, being evil, know how to give good gifts to your children, how much more will your Father from heaven give the good Spirit to them that ask him?"(Luke 11:9-13)

God wants us to express our needs to Him. Of course God knows what we need, but He wants us to entrust ourselves to Him, not to ourselves or to the world. This is an element of trust, of faith. He also wants to hear our thanksgiving, our gratitude. So much will come to a grateful heart. He does not expect perfection but effort. He wants to know of our reliance upon Him and to hear our sorrow for having offended Him when we fall. "My sacrifice, O God, is a contrite spirit; a contrite, humbled heart, O God, you will not scorn."(Ps 51:19) One of our most common and most important prayers should be to ask for wisdom. As men, we are leaders, and we have to make decisions. There are so many ways we could go, decisions we could make with all of them being above evil. But usually there will be only one right choice. We have to be able to assess situations and decisions that will be the best for all concerned. This requires wisdom. A good decision in the eyes of God, one that will be good for the souls of all concerned, will not necessarily be the right decision in the eyes of the world. This is why we need to ask God for guidance and seek counsel from good upright and holy advisors who are also competent in the areas involved.

On the topic of prayer and faith, I would be remiss if I were not to mention the Blessed Virgin Mary and the Holy Rosary. Devotion to our Lady is a basic part of our Catholic Faith. God made her an integral part of His plan of salvation. Of course we do not worship or adore her. That level of reverence is reserved only for the Triune God. That being said, devotion to our Lady should never been seen as weak or feminine. Many powerful and holy men throughout the history of the Church have had a strong devotion to our Lady. She is the Seat of Wisdom and can offer us so much guidance in our daily lives through our prayer. She is also very active in the spiritual combat against Satan. She will guide us in our fight against evil if we ask her. Praying the Rosary (5 decades) daily is a very good practice for all Catholics.

Conduct in Church

Already we are to carry ourselves with greater dignity as Catholic men than the rest of society but when entering into the presence of our Lord we're are going to have to elevate things all the more. As Catholics, we are blessed with a Gift that no other denomination is granted. When we enter into a Catholic Church, the Blessed Sacrament is present. Jesus Christ is present Body, Blood, Soul, and Divinity in Substance, not only in a Spiritual sense, but Substantially present. This is a mystery, not totally comprehensible, but worth of our contemplation and realization.

While in Church (or otherwise in the Presence of the Blessed Sacrament) we should remain silent and focused on our Lord. We are not to talk or visit with anyone unless absolutely necessary, as in to correct a child under our charge or if you are assisting the Priest in the arrangements for the Mass. The time and place to greeting others is not within the Church. We have all week and all day long to be social. This is the only time we have with our Lord. We need to treasure it. This is the only time and place we can acquire the Wisdom and Knowledge that only comes from Christ Himself in His Substantial Presence. There is a reason He gave Himself to us in this Way, so we need to partake of It fully.

If you are like me, you may need some help to stay focused. I can get distracted and my mind can wander to the multitude of things a father and businessman have to handle. Some men can just sit and experience the Presence of the Lord quietly and stay fixed on Him. I have found that I need to stay in active prayer. Of course the highest form of prayer is Holy Mass. When attending Mass we need to pay close attention to what is going on throughout the various parts of the Mass. This is the Way the Lord longed to be worshipped. The Mass is a re-presentation, a making present of the Sacrifice on Calvary again, in the present. This is why it is called the perpetual Sacrifice. It was only done once, but will last until the end of the world. It is always being made present again.

It is a good practice to make regular visits to the Blessed Sacrament reserved in the Tabernacle at Church separately from attending Mass. A good habit for most men is to make a Holy Hour once a week. I have found this practice over time has strengthened me spiritually helping me to stay centered on our Lord and balanced while carrying out the duties of my state in life. During visits to the Blessed Sacrament I like to have prayer books with me as well as spiritual reading material. I of course have the option to stop and meditate on a prayer I am praying or the subject I am reading, but having these materials keeps me engaged and helps me to continue once my meditation on a certain thought has completed.

A Proper Attitude toward Money

A person of faith will live his life in a much different way and from a different paradigm from a person of no faith. A Catholic person will approach life in a different way even from a person of another faith. Again, we believe this is what God wants of us based on the Teachings of Christ in Scripture and handed down through the Apostolic Tradition of the Church.

There is so much materialism in our society today it is difficult to escape its influence. However, our Lord said "No man can serve two masters. For either he will hate the one, and love the other: or he will sustain the one, and despise the other. You cannot serve God and mammon (riches, worldly interests)."(Matt 6:24) Again, God wants our dependence to be on Him, not things of this world. It is so tempting to start to trust in worldly things and money once one acquires some and sees the power that it wields in society. When that temptation comes all we have to do is look at our end. If we look at the elderly who are sick, frail, and weak we will be reminded of the old adage "You can't take it with you." The elderly may have massive fortunes built up, but it cannot buy a fountain of youth or permanence of life on earth. We will all die one day; that's one thing that is definite.

This does not necessarily mean that we all have to live in poverty in order to get to heaven. In that case we would never be able to even gather in a Church. Things in this life cost money. Of course it requires money to build and maintain Church facilities. If a man has no money, how can he build a home for his family and feed them. So the challenge becomes knowing when we are serving God and when we are serving mammon. Obviously there's no clear cut answer to that. Our Lord said "Blessed are the poor in spirit: for theirs is the kingdom of heaven."(Matt 5:3) So we are to be poor in spirit even if we possess some wealth. We cannot let it be our sole purpose in life or our principal purpose. We should have our end as doing God's Will. So whatever wealth God provides for us to acquire by doing good and dealing in a fair and just manner, we are to discern over what He would want us to do with it. Even better, we should have a financial plan to acquire a certain amount of wealth with a future use in mind. This perspective is much different from one who just recklessly seeks to acquire as much money as possible solely for pleasure and possessions.

The discernment of money is particularly challenging for a family man as this is our particular way in participating in our redemption. When Adam and Eve sinned in the Garden of Eden, they were each given a punishment by God, a sentence if you will, that would last the rest of their lives and be perpetuated throughout the entire human race. "To the woman also he said: I will multiply thy sorrows, and thy conceptions: in sorrow shalt thou bring forth children, and thou shalt be under thy husband' s power, and he shall have dominion over thee. And to Adam he said: Because thou hast hearkened to the voice of thy wife, and hast eaten of the tree, whereof I commanded thee that thou shouldst not eat, cursed is the earth in thy work; with labour and toil shalt thou eat thereof all the days of thy life."(Gen 3:16-17) Our sentence as men is to work for a living to provide for a wife and children. We will compassionately hear the needs of our wives and children, and those needs will require money. So this isn't some small incidental or discretionary matter. This is our sustenance. So it would be erroneous for a family man to willing accept or desire poverty. If a man chooses such, he should remain single.

In matters of time and money we should put our families first before our own selfish interests and desires. We need to make it a priority that all of their needs are met. Ideally, the man should provide for his family, and his wife should stay home caring for the home and children, as mentioned in chapter 2. Instead of a man working so that he can have leisure, he works because his family depends on him. We can see from Scripture that this is the way God originally intended for this to work. When we do this, we can live out the Church's teaching on being open to life and welcoming children in our families. It is so prevalent for Catholic couples to use contraception, which is a mortal sin(CCC ¶2399) that could result in the loss of their souls for all of eternity, because the wife has a career and a baby would be an interference.

> According to Dr. Janet E. Smith quoting a study done by economist Robert Michael, when a couple has a baby within the first 2 years of marriage and another one within the next 2 years...those marriages will last a lot longer than those who don't. When women have babies early in the marriage they become financially dependent upon their husbands...Now women are delaying childbearing until 4 or 5 years into the marriage. By that time a woman

> is established in her own career, she's financially independent and so if the marriage goes badly, there are no children around, and she can kick him out. Even if they do have children, she's established herself in a career and she can take care of the children.[17]

All of the intimate acts between a husband and wife should be open to conception (CCC ¶2366), and a stay at home full-time mother is best positioned to welcome a baby.

Leading a family requires sacrifice. Anything that is worth anything does. Those who aspire to greatness in their fields, whether it be music, sports, etc., have to sacrifice their own comforts and leisure to work at their craft. The same rule applies to family. Yet family is a much higher calling than these other pursuits. Our work should be at the service of our families, not vice versa. This element of sacrifice is right in line with our Catholic Faith. Our Lord tells us, "If any man will come after me, let him deny himself, and take up his cross, and follow me."(Matt 16:24) This is not sacrifice in terms of a drudgery or nuisance. It is giving up something menial for a higher calling. We only need so much leisure. God's ratio was to work six days and rest one. (cf Gen 2:2) He gives us that same ratio. We are to be creative and constructive the vast majority of the time. So we should make ourselves available to our families, spending time there leading them and directing them.

---

[17]Dr. Janet E. Smith "Contraception: Why Not" (Federal Way, WA: Trinity Formation Resources, 2004) (audio CD)

The overall life of a Catholic is a penitential life in fact. It is a common practice to offer sacrifices we make in reparation for our sins and the sins of the world. The Church works with our human nature. Our nature is to pass through intervals, long and short: 16 waking hours, 8 sleeping hours; 6 days work, 1 day rest; 4 seasons—spring, summer, fall, winter. The Church gives us seasons for penance—Lent and Advent, but then also requires a penitential day each week, Friday. We should make sure to observe all Fridays during the year as days of penance.[18] The United States Bishops give first preference to abstinence from meat as the penance for Fridays.[19]

Finally the attitude of a Catholic man should be trust in and dependence on God. This means we do our part, and God will do His. Once we've been responsible and done our best we need to trust in God's Will, Divine Providence that the outcome is for the best. St. Augustine put it this way: "Pray as if everything depended on God and work as if everything depended on you."(CCC ¶2834)

---

[18] Code of Canon Law c.1250 *Code of Canon Law Latin-English Edition* (Washington, DC: Canon Law Society of America, 1983) p. 447

[19] United States Catholic Bishops, "Pastoral Statement on Penance and Abstinence" *United States Conference of Catholic Bishops* November 18, 1966 ¶24

The first setting in which faith enlightens the human city is the family. I think first and foremost of the stable union of man and woman in marriage. This union is born of their love as a sign and presence of God's own love, and of the acknowledgment and acceptance of the goodness of sexual differentiation, whereby spouses can become one flesh (cf. Gen 2:24) and are enabled to give birth to a new life, a manifestation of the creator's goodness, wisdom, and loving plan.[20]

Pope Francis
(Encyclical Letter *Lumen Fidei*
[nos. 52-53], June 29, 2013)

---

[20] Theresa Aletheia Noble, FSP and Donna Giaimo, FSP, Give Us This Day our Daily Love (Boston; Pauline Books & Media, 2015), p 23

PART II – USING OUR TOOLS

CHAPTER 9

Independence/Interdependence
Brothers, stop being childish in your thinking. In respect
to evil be like infants, but in your thinking be mature.
(1Cor.14:20)

Independence is the ability to provide for yourself
without parental assistance growing to interdependence
with other adults mutually providing value to one
another.

Now that we've enumerated and thoroughly
analyzed the tools we possess as men, let's move into
putting them to use as we move from an adolescent male
into becoming a man considering his overall basic
purpose culminating in leading a family. According to
James Stenson, educational consultant, "The most
effective fathers and mothers I've known all seem to be
moved by a strategic, far-seeing vision: *they see*
themselves raising adults, not children."[21] So, in our
case, on the topic of males-boys, they are to become
men. The goal is to move from the haven of the home
and the dependence upon the parents to independence,
being able to support themselves without the assistance
of anyone else.

The concept of independence and
interdependence on a continuum comes from Steven

---

[21] James B. Stenson, <u>Father, the Family Protector</u> (New York:
Scepter Publishers, Inc., 2004) p. 45

Covey's book <u>The 7 Habits of Highly Effective People</u>. His 7 Habits framework is an excellent tool to use in personal development and maturity. They break down this way: the tools of independence are: (1) be proactive, (2) begin with the end in mind, (3) put first things first, (4) think win-win, (5) seek first to understand, then to be understood, (6) synergize, and (7) sharpen the saw.[22] If we look at the first 3 tools, or habits, we see that these move an individual from dependence to independence. The next 3 move a person from independence to interdependence. This book is a highly recommended resource for men of all ages to assist in personal development toward working most effectively with others in today's society. Just reading through these habits, you can see the powerful concepts that are assembled to build a man up and to move him toward building others up.

This is an important progression for the man of today. We no longer live the time of tenure and lifetime appointments or careers. Today men have to prove themselves every day. We have to produce results that matter. The men that get jobs, hold jobs, advance in their careers, and supervise and lead others are those who learn how to work with others and get the best out of them. The days are gone when men can suppress others in order to maintain their positions. About the only place that still works may be in some government positions. But for the most part in most occupations men will occupy in private business, men must learn to work with and assist others in excelling. There's a quote I've

---

[22] Stephen R. Covey, <u>The 7 Habits of Highly Effective People: Powerful Lessons in Personal Change</u> (New York, NY: Simon and Schuster, 1989) p.60

heard from Zig Ziglar that I often recall "You can get everything you want in life if you help enough other people get what they want." Jim Rohn gave the analogy of 2 types of men both of who wanted the largest building in town. One man set out to build a building taller than all the others. The other went around tearing down all the other buildings larger than his. What type of man should we aspire to be? Fortunately our society and our Faith encourage us to be the man that builds others up not tears them down.

Independence

Similar to the approach recommended by Steven Covey of beginning with the end in mind, I have taught my children especially as they are getting older and looking toward relationships to make of themselves someone to give to others or do for others. Bring something to the table in all relationships, not only toward marriage, but also in careers, friendships, or religious vocations. There has to be an equal exchange of value or some way we each contribute in our relationships. We get into relationships because of the synergies produced by them. For instance in a family, the husband and wife together will contribute more than they could separately. We can see this in families where the parents are divorced. There are still 2 people in the broken relationship, but together could contribute more to the family.

We may often hear of trying to find that right person that completes us or makes us whole. But I believe that is a big mistake people make in relationships. Before a man can move into healthy relationships, he has to have a certain amount of self-assurance and self-identity. Even in friendships, we can all think of someone who uses others or who has even used us for our possessions or as a crutch because of something he is lacking. We can see how this is weak and can be destructive to all involved.

When we practice virtue, we begin to move toward self-realization, we gain self-control. We start to gain some mastery over our flesh and our spirit starts controlling. We stop serving the body and have the body serve us in doing good. This is where using the tools outlined in Part I start to take hold and take effect. For instance, consider the first tool of strength. Can you see how possessing strength can lend to someone's independence? Regarding something as basic as *stamina for work*, when a man shows consistency on the job and learns his trade and performs it to the needs of his employer, customer, or client, he brings great value to that relationship. This was one of the many revelations I received in listening to Jim Rohn, entrepreneur, author and motivational speaker: We should focus on bringing value. In his case, he would say to bring value to the marketplace. But we could also say to bring value to relationships. In his case he would say that this is how one can generate more income, by being more valuable or doing a more valuable task. In relationships, we contribute more when we can be of greater value. This is why Rohn would also say to "work harder on yourself than you do on your job." When we work to perfect our skills and our character, we can stand on our own two feet without the assistance of parents or partners.

As we move toward independence it is critical to start to envision a life purpose. The immense amount of energy and drive that is generated by the knowledge of a purpose is difficult to describe. For instance, if a man knows that he wants to have a family some day, he will look at what is required of a family man. He has to be strong, reliable, astute, alert, and of great moral character and virtue. He will go to work on these attributes in order to achieve his goal. However, if a man just doesn't know what he wants to do with his life or if he just lives for sense pleasure, does he really have any reason to get out of bed in the morning? Does he have to learn anything or develop any virtue? Of course he doesn't.

I remember knowing this part of my life purpose as early as 7th grade Catechism class with my closest friend's mom as the teacher, Mrs. Lois. Of course, the catechism teachers would encourage us all to consider a vocation to the Priesthood or religious life. But since I knew the teacher, I could be quite open and frank. That would have been when I was about 12 years old. Even then I told Mrs. Lois in the presence of the whole class that I thought the Priesthood was a great and high calling, but I knew I wanted to get married. Likewise, since she knew me, she knew she could be candid and light-hearted with me and asked aloud in front of everyone "Now Raylan, who is going to marry you?" Of course I admitted that I didn't know who but I knew that's what I wanted to do.

That ambition only grew stronger as I grew older. I saw some of the weaknesses in families that I thought I would try to avoid. I saw some good things in other families I would want to achieve. Those were all rough impressions in my later teenage years obviously surrounded by the awe of discovering the beauty and mystery of girls. But they became refined as the picture of my future came more into focus.

But having these aspirations drove me to a great amount of discipline in my studies in college that would lead to a degree necessary for my career. All the while I could observe classmates skipping classes, not completing assignments, and making no preparations for examinations. What was the difference between me and them? It was a vision, a purpose.

Another thing that will drive one to independence is need. In my case, I knew that I had only one chance to get a degree. There was no room for error. I had limited financial resources and limited time. The first two summers of college I spent working on offshore workboats, a somewhat dangerous job. But it paid well for someone with no skills. This created a laser focus for me to seize the one opportunity I had to achieve a goal that was a stepping stone toward a larger purpose.

All these are examples of independence in themselves and movement toward even greater independence. A man has a vision, a goal of where he wants his life to go, and he sets himself on that path. When he has that laser focus, get out of his way because he will not be stopped but by the Will of God. It is a tremendous thing to experience and a tremendous thing to observe.

Interdependence

Everyone has a pretty good understanding of independence, but the concept of interdependence may be a bit difficult to grasp. Again, this is the basis of the beginning of substantive relationships. People become dependent on each other as each brings a respective value for a specific purpose. We see this a lot with partnerships in business. One partner may be good from the technical or operational side of the business and needs a partner who is well versed in the business side. Often each of the two can't work without the other, or they can't work as well independently.

To move from independence to interdependence though we have a critical element that has to come into play in considering the other party to the relationship, and this element is very Catholic in nature: respect. "Respect for the human person entails respect for the rights that flow from his dignity as a creature. These rights are prior to society and must be recognized by it. They are the basis of the moral legitimacy of every authority..." (CCC¶1930) This respect manifests itself in many ways in order for the relationship to reach its potential: sensitivity, kindness, appreciation, communication, and sacrifice (of personal preferences and comforts, not compromise of principles). We can see the Catholic character of all of these manifestations especially in the way of sacrifice. We recall that one of the greatest commands Christ gave us was to love one another. (John 13:34) These manifestations are marks of brotherly charity and will embolden all relationships.

Interdependence is a step well above the concept of acquaintance or friendship. With the concept of interdependence there is a "working relationship" that can produce a greater good. To achieve this level of interaction we have to continue to work on ourselves. Again, let's refer back to our tools in Part I of this book. Let's consider commitment this time. If we have developed the principle of commitment, we feel an obligation to the people of our interdependence.

I currently have this type of collaboration with an associate in an online Apostolate called Fix the Family. The endeavor started out as a You Tube channel, and has grown to a website and blog moving toward an educational media company. My contributions to the project have been content knowledge, speaking ability, writing ability, public relations, marketing, and light technology capabilities. His contributions have been camera work (still and moving), extensive camera equipment knowledge, video direction, editing and production, extensive technology capability, and content knowledge. When we began making videos for airing on You Tube, it was an immense amount of work, and we both had a lot to learn. We had to practice a great amount of patience with each other and to be respectful of each other as we learned the ropes. Over time both of our abilities in this undertaking have improved as we have encouraged each other along.

In addition to the mutual encouragement, we also feel accountable to each other. If we have an appointment to record a video, I don't want to waste his time by being unprepared. I want to know my material so that the video shoot can run smoothly. Likewise, he is respectful of me in arriving timely for appointments to shoot and working very diligently in making our product professional and polished. The synergy that is present in this relationship is very powerful and productive. Additionally, when we have this kind of synergy present and working, it becomes very inspiring creating a momentum to steadily continue in the endeavor. We feed productive enthusiasm off of each other. These types of relationships take effort to build, but they are very effective in accomplishing significant results.

Providing

A significant practical application of this concept of independence and interdependence is first to become self-supporting with the eventual goal of being able to support a family autonomously without the wife having to produce an income. When we are young and dependent upon our parents, we aren't required to exert ourselves to the extent we must when we are independent or when we have others dependent upon us. That is acceptable and even good during the time of adolescence when the main objective is learning and character development. It is also very healthy to have a balanced innocent enjoyable youth that includes study, work, and play.

But as we mature with each passing year, we should be able to handle greater and greater responsibilities. This is the natural growing-up process that men are supposed to go through. The first step for a young man in this is to move from dependence upon his parents to being able to provide for himself. Obviously this will happen at different time frames depending on the young man's calling in life, his occupation. If he is called to be a professional of some sort such as a doctor, lawyer, nurse, etc, he will require a college degree. If he has to go to college, his time frame for becoming independent will likely be longer.

This is actually a bit of a disadvantage to the man with such a calling as he has to delay the ability to begin his career and generate income. Also he will experience an outlay of funds toward payment of tuition to the institution of higher learning he will attend. This is part of the price he has to pay for the duty to which he is called. All too often today, a college education is seen as a golden ticket that will guarantee a perfect future. Emotionally charged (but meaningless) statements like "they can't take your education away from you" are often bandied about. Statistics of the higher incomes produced by degreed students are published far and wide in order to keep enrollments up at these institutions. While those statistics may be accurate, there are also limited numbers of positions that require those degrees. So, only the most qualified graduates (or those that fit the gender or race employment quota requirements of the business) end up working in those positions. The point here is that while a college degree in some cases may allow for a greater income, there is no guarantee that a graduate will find a job in the field he desires.

A young man has to be discerning about his vocation toward an occupation for this very reason. He could waste four years of precious productive time as well as thousands of dollars in tuition only to end up in a job that never required a degree to begin with. The job could very well be something he enjoys immensely and pays well, but he doesn't need the degree. Regardless, the vast majority of people will say, "You can't take it from him." We should be able to see how empty of a statement this is. For these reason, instead of college being viewed as a vital step in a person's development and education, college should be viewed more as an optional step only carefully to be taken if reasonably seen as a requirement for the future occupation of the young man.

A much better route for many young men is a skilled labor or technical field. Often a trade school or community college education can accomplish the necessary targeted learning requirements before joining up into those disciplines. There are still a few occupations that can be learned on the job with apprentice-type training, but those often don't pay well enough to support a family. Regardless of the specific occupation, a man should seek to find the occupation that will most aptly use his strengths and talents.

I am very familiar with the mineral exploration and extraction environment, what we on the gulf coast refer to as "the oilfield." The number of service occupations surrounding this industry is difficult to describe. These jobs are men's jobs, ones that require heavy technical equipment and large heavy-duty trucks. These are the things many men like and gravitate toward. It is our element. It is often said to get into an occupation doing something you like so that you'll enjoy your work. I would agree with that; we should go with our strengths. But I would temper that by saying that with the day to day grind of work, every "career" ends up being a job. Even if you do enjoy what you do, it still remains drudgery. That being said I've been around people who literally hate their job, and that's really is somewhat of hell on earth. So, yes find something you enjoy doing that resonates with your masculinity but also can generate a significant income.

This is not to be confused with simply going after what you "love" or your passion. I had an ambition to be a professional runner but did not possess the talent. There are many who have artistic talents that make the huge mistake of trying to make a living with them.

Musicians and artists rarely can ever make a basic living with those jobs. It's either feast or famine. If someone makes it big in these types of fields, it is usually not practical for family life with the lifestyle that goes along with it. So men who simply want to develop these types of passionate pursuits should probably not marry.

Again, what we're talking about here is toward the pursuit of a family life. So the job as a provider has to be one that will make a significant income while still allowing for significant time with the family. That would mean returning home most nights. Once the occupation is chosen, a man needs to apply himself to it vigorously in becoming proficient with it. This will take years. A man who is becoming independent needs to buckle down and work through the learning curve of the occupation. He will have a family depending on him for it. He needs to approach it this way.

Ideally he should be well into his career once he decides to get married. As mentioned in chapter 2, men should approach their work as if they will be the sole provider for the family. This is a mistake that most young couples make. They assume they will be a dual-career family but once they start having children, the wife often no longer wants to work. This is a compounded problem when the wife has gone to college and feels like she has to use her hard-earned degree or if she has student loans to repay. I have heard of numerous couples in this conundrum seeing they have been deceived by an agenda that promised so much and delivered so little. While the couple may both have jobs, they are at odds with a balanced family life. Some of these couples I see find a way to courageously bite the bullet and make the financial sacrifices for the husband to work and pay off his wife's student loans so that she can be the wife and mother their family needs. This is a grand example of independence and interdependence of a real man.

This is where manhood today can really take hold. Ideally, if he knows this ahead of time, he won't make this mistake and won't have to compromise financially. But he does have to be prepared to sacrifice. The reality is that as he is going through the learning curve in any occupation, he will not make as much money as his experienced co-workers and supervisors. This is the quandary faced by all young families. With the needs of a growing family having babies, there are many necessary expenses that come with them. The key word here is necessary. Despite the challenge of having to meet these expenses, a man along with his wife will often have to sacrifice some optional material things (luxuries) for the huge nonmonetary benefit of his wife staying home with their children and raising them instead of turning them over to strangers in daycare. We have to be prudent and vigilant in this because the society we live in sees many optional material things as necessary. It is amazing when we realize the things we can do without when there is a greater good at stake.

Probably the greatest savings a young couple starting out can achieve would come from sharing a single vehicle. I recall in my own personal finances that the cost of operating and maintaining a vehicle is quite a significant portion of a worker's income. We had an interesting episode with that. I had a large repair bill to pay for our car when I had just started my first job and we had our first infant child. We were out of money, but I did not want to go to my parents. I had to go to a finance company, pledge personal assets (which were very few and meager), and pay a usurious interest rate. My employer paid a bonus for passing the CPA exam, so when I passed it and got the bonus, I paid off the loan. Also, many Catholic parents want to send their children to Catholic schools, many of which are marginally Catholic. Regardless, this expense is very disproportionate to income so often requires couples to limit the number of children they will have in order to afford them. A much more practical option is for the mother to homeschool the children which goes hand-in-hand with mothering them and welcoming the children God will send them. Of course there are other optional things and luxuries families can do without like cable television, electronic devices, smart phones/i-phones, name-brand clothes, etc.

Another aspect of this that is often overlooked with regard to the husband being the sole provider is that it frees him to fully apply himself to his work while on the job. When a couple has a dual-career arrangement, they each have to compromise their career for the other. Since neither is primarily committed to the children, they will often have to take turns in who is going to pick up them up or take them to the doctor or to school. When a man has these concerns in the back of his mind and has to leave work early, his co-workers that don't have these issues are still on the job furthering themselves and developing in their occupations. This creates an immense amount of tension in the marriage. This tension further compromises both of their abilities to perform well at work. With such a dilemma, women will often want to stop having children. However, the beautiful teaching of the Church always unites marriage with the acceptance of children. "Fecundity is a gift, an end of marriage, for conjugal love naturally tends to be fruitful. A child does not come from outside as something added on to the mutual love of the spouses, but springs from the very heart of that mutual giving, as its fruit and fulfillment. So the Church, which is 'on the side of life,' teaches that 'it is necessary that each and every marriage act remain ordered per se to the procreation of human life.'" (CCC¶2366) So, many times the dual-career arrangement when taken on unnecessarily and purposefully for materialistic or worldly purposes can result in an occasion of sin. It often leads the couple to the use of artificial contraception, which is a mortal sin. "The regulation of births represents one of the aspects of responsible fatherhood and motherhood. Legitimate intentions on the part of the spouses do not justify recourse to morally unacceptable means (for example, direct sterilization or contraception)."(CCC¶2399) We also must be cautious with use of acceptable natural means of *postponing* pregnancy for illicit purposes. "A particular aspect of this responsibility concerns the *regulation of procreation*. For just reasons, spouses may wish to space the births of their children. It is their duty to make certain that their desire is not motivated by selfishness but is in conformity with the generosity appropriate to responsible parenthood." (CCC¶2368) The dual-career arrangement is a vicious cycle that often leads to an end to something, either the arrangement or the marriage. All too often it is the marriage.

But when his wife is at home with the children, he has far fewer worries. She is safe at home with their children. The children are being cared for by the person best qualified to do so. They are all content. They see the beauty in this life and their children and want to have more. He can put in his full day of work focusing on his tasks since he doesn't have these outside concerns. Since he has been productive, he can leave work at a reasonable time to return home to his family to spend the evening with them.

It is so important that we get this right for the next generation. We need to be forward thinking in this most basic area of life. This is a critical mistake that so many young couples are making all the time. Good Catholic parents are advising their children to go the dual-career route under the guise of there being no alternative, regardless of the detrimental results we continue to see around us. This is one area where Catholic manhood really needs to take hold and flourish.

CHAPTER 10

Relationships

Charm is deceptive and beauty fleeting; the woman who fears the LORD is to be praised.
(Prov.31:30)

Relationships with the opposite sex need to be sought and formed with forethought and purpose to the proper ends.

The natural progression from independence to interdependence is the road toward building valuable relationships. We have all had friends, and we have all had acquaintances. We should know the difference. Then we have classmates in school and coworkers at work. Some of these relationships are stronger than others. We can identify with some people better than others based on personality, interests, and priorities. We all naturally like and dislike certain things. We may have a certain interest in music that others will find distasteful. We may enjoy certain types of entertainment that others won't. I recall some young ladies that I knew as a teenager that said they would never like to get dressed up in a dress and go out to eat at a nice restaurant. They would much prefer to put on a pair of jeans or shorts and go to McDonald's. I knew for my personal tastes and interests, these young ladies would not interest me. I knew another young lady who had a strong interest in having a certain type of dog. I didn't have an interest in dogs. There again I could see how something of that much of an importance to someone could be a conflict to another in a relationship.

Just by considering these few things we can see how complex relationships can be. These may all seem to be trivial things, but we have to consider the realities of day to day life and the amount of commitment we are willing to make to things for the sake of another. When a young person starts to have an interest in relationships that would go beyond friendships (here we will only consider heterosexual/natural relationships) they need to begin to see these things of interest that they can share with others.

Poor Beginnings

During the period of adolescence, these interests obviously start to heighten, and these young people become very interested in relationships. All too often because of a permissive culture today (often made up of permissive parents), these young people get involved in serious relationships way too early. I personally recall the introduction to exclusive dating amongst my classmates beginning when I was in sixth grade. So at that time I would have been about 11 years old. This was around when girls were started to physically mature into young ladies. I distinctly remember noticing this in seventh grade when I would have been 12 years old. I have vivid memories of the onset of puberty and first noticing girls as more than just friends. I recall the start of dances at school right around this time as well.

Now all this might seem innocent, but let's look at what was happening in the culture. I would also recall seeing old movies where young people of similar ages or possibly a little older in high school where the storyline would include them going to a dance. But the dances in these old movies looked nothing like the dances I was seeing. In those movies, the kids were having fun dancing to lively wholesome music being played by a live acoustic band. Sure, the plot would include young people of either gender nervous about whom they'd take to the dance. But what I was seeing were classmates get into serious "committed" relationships as though they were each other's property. At dances, instead of lively and fun, I'd see kids together in the dark with flashing lights and blaring pop music played on a sound system with the sounds of suggestive lyrics. By the time the high school stage came along, that was compounded with alcohol and many of the couples were obviously sexually active.

I recall that by the time we had a senior prom it was an overnight event where many of the kids would gather and "crash" for the rest of the night or into the wee hours of the morning. That would have been during the 1980's. What was the result of this type of casual serial monogamy and intense dating often with an assumed sexual commitment? Well, you're seeing it in the 40 something's of today. We have a majority of marriages that ended in divorce. According to Dr. Janet E. Smith, "In the 1960's 1 out of 4 marriages in the United States ended in divorce. At the turn of the century in the United States it was well under 10% of marriages that ended in divorce. By the mid-1970's it was 1 out of 2 marriages ending in divorce. It stayed right about there...but about 1 out of 2 marriages are now ending in divorce."[23] Did any of these people

---

[23] Dr. Janet E. Smith "Contraception: Why Not" (Federal Way, WA: Trinity Formation Resources, 2004) (audio CD)

understand how to have a meaningful relationship at such a young and emotionally tumultuous stage in their lives? Apparently they did not. Many commitments entered into during the high school ages did not last. I can imagine there must have been tremendous heartbreak as they ended and the couple went their separate ways on to the next stage of their lives. How much attachment must they have formed having been together for so long and having given away such a personal part of themselves! I only have to look at the Facebook pages of these friends I once knew or the photos of the class reunions and the empirical divorce statistics start to bear familiar faces. It is very sad to see. Many continue on later in life bouncing in and out of relationships further in order to avoid isolation.

If we stop and think about this phenomenon rationally we can see how damaging this is. Young people at the most vulnerable stages of their lives continue to be allowed almost with no restraint to enter into very emotionally and physically intimately intense relationships . Parental involvement has gradually been eroded away, and the school system exercises an inordinate amount of influence over the children. Parents almost ignorantly continue to turn their own duties and responsibilities toward their children over to the government. In the long run, it is the children who suffer the most. We must learn from the permissiveness of our own upbringing and the poor results it bore.

A Better Approach to Dating-Courtship

As a result of these very sordid outcomes, some wise parents have decided to take their role more seriously and not give their children over to the culture.

They have exercised their proper responsibility in the formation and guidance of their children beyond just the toddler and childhood stages but on into adolescence by delaying and limiting their involvement in exclusive relationships. The old custom of courtship began to surface again in the 1990s, as evidenced by Joshua Harris's book I Kissed Dating Goodbye,[24] along with a significant push by various Christian denominations, most notably Catholics, for chastity amongst teenagers and young adults with Jason Evert's books Pure Love [25] and If You Really Loved Me: 100 Questions on Dating, Relationships and Sexual Purity.[26]

I encourage young people including my own children to delay getting into exclusive relationships until it is reasonably possible to get married. So if we compare that to my experience as a child, in sixth grade obviously no one is ready to get married. The problem with starting relationships so young is even though they may be totally innocent (which many aren't), the progression toward serious relationships is initiated. Once we are titillated with the exclusive gushy affections of another, we naturally want to move forward to heightened stages. It is no wonder why someone starting to get involved in relationships in elementary school would be sexually active in high school.

---

[24] Joshua Harris, I Kissed Dating Goodbye (Colorado Springs, CO; Multnomah Books, 1997)

[25] Jason Evert, Pure Love (San Diego; Catholic Answers Press, 1999)

[26] Jason Evert, If You Really Loved Me: 100 Questions on Dating, Relationships and Sexual Purity (El Cajon, CA; Catholic Answers, Inc., 2002)

Courting and courtship can have different rules or standards for different groups or communities. But the basic idea is to save exclusive relationships for the later stage when preparing for marriage. So what does one do until then? As mentioned in Chapter 6, kids need to be allowed to have an innocent childhood and period of adolescence. There are many enjoyable activities young people of both genders can do together in groups without having to pair up. That is actually for the more mature stages of life when things get "serious." There should be some sense of frivolity for teens on balance before the more serious stages of life demand that games be an occasional break from the grind.

So when is a young person ready to court? I'm sure that's the question begged by this whole discussion. It's rather obvious that the answer would be my favorite "it depends." It depends largely on the person, their circumstances, their maturity level, and their ambitions. I know a young lady who was married around 19 years old even in today's culture. This was no rebellious young lady looking for refuge away from an abusive home, like one might assume based on age alone. She married an older stable man and immediately began to start a family with him. They are of like mind and were ready to make that step and commitment together. Is that the typical age? Probably not. As said much of the frivolity has not run its course by that time.

Typically once someone has had enough "fun" and all the running of the circuit starts to get old, a guy or a gal is going to want to "settle down." That's probably the time when serious relationships can start. They are going to be in the right frame of mind looking for the right kind of person to spend the rest of their lives with and to unite with to have and raise children. Of course THIS is the basis for true love and true marriage. When one is just interested in fun and being entertained, a companion for that alone will likely not be the one he'll want to spend the rest of his life with. He will begin to desire a person with different attributes when the status of lifelong partner enters the picture. This is the proper maturity level and focus on priorities for the time to begin making this all important decision.

Ideally, one would not have to go through more than a few exclusive relationships before arriving at a good match. This can cut down on the emotional turmoil that is naturally to result from the dating game. One only wants to expose their heart and deepest personal longings to the fewest number of people as possible. Still, if a man starts to court a young lady after having chosen her based on important traits and compatibility but then finds that she may not be the right one for him, he should not delay in breaking things off or voicing his concerns. Often men will just continue on in the relationship even into marriage while knowing things are wrong long before the wedding. I've seen this happen more than once to men close to me, and the marriages were very brief in duration.

Once a couple does start to court, they can probably soon tell whether or not they are truly compatible and if they should proceed. I know a young man who at a fairly young adult age, especially by today's standards began courting a young lady under the proper circumstances discussed here. He shared that before he got too emotionally involved with her that he clearly outlined and communicated to her what his expectations of the roles of each of them in married life would be, which are the traditional roles that the Church has always taught, that we promote in this book and that he saw growing up in his own family. Again, he did this in a very pragmatically serious and unemotional way. Once the young lady understood what his expectations were, she agreed and they continued on with their courtship and married. They are a very responsible and mature couple with a growing young family. This is the way courtship toward marriage is supposed to work.

So we see the emphasis here to having the relationships geared in the direction where they should be, toward marriage. Otherwise the relationships are for convenience, pleasure, and use of the other person if they take on a serious nature and become exclusive. It is limited to a couple just being an "item," someone to attend functions with and to accompany in social gatherings. So, it makes sense that when this is the limitation, that this should only involve adults who have arrived at a place of maturity where they are emotionally independent and prepared to offer themselves to the other. They would also be equipped to have something of value in themselves to offer the other in a permanent relationship, not looking for another to "complete" them as persons.

CHAPTER 11

Intimate Companionship

To find a wife is to find happiness, a favor granted by the LORD. (Prov 18:22)

Finding your intimate companion could be the most important thing you do in life because it is for a lifetime.

When it comes to relationships, this is what everybody seems to want, intimate companionship. This is a term that I coined myself that describes the type of relationship that I have with my wife. We have all had companions to one degree or another. A companion is one with whom we share common interests. They enjoy being together. Often it doesn't matter what they are doing; they just enjoy each other's company. Each of us probably had a best friend as a kid who was this type of companion.

Then there is intimacy. Intimacy is beyond two people having sex out of mere physical attraction. Intimacy starts with the sharing of one's feelings, emotions, desires, and dreams. It would progress into the sharing of one's deepest self. This is actually what is supposed to happen between a couple during the advanced stages of courting and into engagement. Often when two people share this much about themselves they begin to desire to be physically intimate. Even during engagement a couple is to resist acting on these desires until they have finally taken the vows of matrimony. An engaged couple could still legitimately end their relationship and end up marrying someone else. God designed sexual intimacy to be part of a permanent commitment of marriage since children can naturally be conceived when it is shared. "Sexuality is ordered to the conjugal love of man and woman. In marriage the physical intimacy of the spouses becomes a sign and pledge of spiritual communion. Marriage bonds between baptized persons are sanctified by the sacrament." (CCC¶2360) Children are to be born into a loving family with a mother and a father who will remain together for life and raise them.

Finding "Her"

This is the ultimate for most males at the young adult stage. They may put it off, but it's always in the back of their minds. When is "she" going to present herself? I recall agonizing over this during the college days wishing to meet a good match, one who shared my vision of life and who wanted a similar future. At the same time, I had plans. There were things I wanted to do, places I wanted to go. I started out dating later than most of my peers, not until the last couple of years of high school. Those relationships were shallow and didn't show any prospect of anything long-term. Of course, following the world, that was not the intent. Those were mostly companionships, someone with whom to be an "item" and with whom to attend functions.

Moving into the college years, I gained that focus of seeing more of what I wanted out of life and could see that girls just out and about in society wouldn't be a good fit. My faith had always been important to me so I got involved with the Catholic center on campus. The girls who were also involved there had their faith as a priority as well, or so it seemed. I could see things starting to take shape there. But at the same time, I started to notice that some of these girls would profess that their faith was important but didn't act as such. The whole time here, I'm recognizing things that are important to me in an intimate companion.

But the waiting to find "her" seemed forever, and I'd never really know how fit of a match I'd find. So, I would do things to try to impress certain girls that attracted me. I would try to gain their attention by participating in similar secular interests. I remember putting on certain popular music while making a phone call so they would hear it playing in the background. The urge to impress seemed a necessary part of the process. At the same time, although seeking to find that person, I wasn't going to sit still until I found her. I knew I'd have to graduate and get on with life. I wanted to work for one of the large national firms and travel, see the rest of the country.

Then she appeared. Missy was involved with the Catholic center on campus long before I had arrived there. She's almost three years older than me. I had known her distantly for a couple of years before realizing she had an attraction to me. She was one whose faith I would have expected to be genuine. She had the respect of her peers. She was always referred to as one with a "soft heart." I had respect for her from afar. We were in a group setting one evening with some other students who frequented the center. She playfully indicated an interest toward me. Since she was a bit older and so well respected, I was totally caught off guard. But at the same time, she was not one I felt I needed to impress. As we talked over the next days and weeks and months, and got to know each other better on a more personal level, I began to fall in love. It was her heart. She had the most beautiful heart, and still does. But wait, I had all these plans. It wasn't time yet. Even for a short while I balked at the idea of where this was going. She was one I could love forever, but there were others who still attracted me that I would have wanted to date. But it would not be. The time was right before I would go off further into the world and possibly make some huge regrettable mistakes. I had been prepared for this moment, this woman.

If I had to suggest anything about "finding her," it would be to really know her as a friend or acquaintance first. Then she should be someone you're totally comfortable around. You don't have to impress; you don't have to put on airs. You can genuinely be yourself. It has to be someone you would feel you always knew with whom you'd want to spend forever. She would stand the test of time as you get to know each other, and you wouldn't compromise the important things you want. She would be that someone you could really love forever.

Decision and Commitment

If we want to know how God intended marriage to be, we just have to trace it back to the beginning. Look at how God created Adam and Eve in the beginning in the Garden of Eden. (Gen 2:18 et al) They were alone together in a natural paradise. Don't we see couples almost trying to recreate this scene on their honeymoons? It is a natural desire of ours because this was what God intended for us. Due to the fall of Adam and Eve and sin entering the world, we will never experience it fully. But if we nurture our marriages, we can experience glimpses of it. "In the joys of their love and family life he gives them here on earth a foretaste of the wedding feast of the Lamb." (CCC¶1642)

To have and maintain intimate companionship requires a decision and a commitment. Personally, when I describe my relationship with my wife, I steer clear of referring to her as my "best friend." Because of the physical intimacy we are designed anatomically to share I think of her more as my "girlfriend" or my "woman." I don't mean that in a possessive sense, but in a sense of awe, similar to the way Adam responded when he first saw his wife Eve. There was a sense of awe of mystery in the being who was "bone of his bones and flesh of his flesh" (Gen 2:23) yet was creatively opposite and complementary to him physically. Since we as men are very visual by nature, we could imagine that scene of him first laying eyes upon his beautiful bride. Then God's first <u>command</u>, not suggestion, to them was to be fruitful and multiply. (cf Gen 1:28) He wanted them to be intimate, but not just for themselves but to love in such a way that would bring forth new life, not just any life but another life that could bear an immortal soul.

I made the decision since before we were married that no matter what (for better or for worse) we were going to have a passionate marriage. Personally, I am a romantic so that backed up my reasoning. I wanted to be "in love" with my wife my whole life. So this means that regardless of what would happen with us as our life together would take its course, I would still desire and take pleasure in her inside and out.

It started with a decision, but then I had to follow that decision up with a commitment. When another attractive lady catches my eye, as will happen since I am a normal man, I will still make the decision to be attracted to her. When she is in poor health, I will still make the decision to cherish her. As she begins to age, I will still make the decision to be in love with and to desire her. My actions do not change due to age or because of any waning of feelings or emotion. I realize that I can't trust my feelings as they are fickle. If my feelings are no longer stimulated by my wife, I realize it must be because I am distracted and not paying attention to her. I can decide to see her imperfections or her beauty. There is a saying that each person that is married has about an 80:20 ratio of favorable traits to unfavorable. This goes for the husband and wife. We can decide and commit to focus on the 80 or the 20. I have chosen to focus on the 80 and still love the 20.

Part of that commitment is to preserve her youth and vitality. This was a significant factor in deciding that we would suffice on my income alone. It was difficult at first, and we had to sacrifice some material things. But those things were optional, and today since I have been able to focus on my career without her having a competing one, we can afford many more material things we like. Yet we realized that her having babies and not going to the daily grind of a job would support her feminine physiological needs. It is true and has borne itself out. A woman's body was made to have babies, not to endure the stress of a job. Unfortunately, some women are forced into this or feel like they need it. But I see many women who are physically worn out in appearance from the stresses and strains of working outside the home.

The commitment also is in the way I choose to see her and treat her. One of my pet peeves is to hear a man refer to his wife as his "old lady." I realize for most of them, that they are just picking on their wives. But women are sensitive emotional beings. The motivators talk about the importance of the meaning of words. I recall Zig Ziglar telling a story about being overweight, but he had playfully trained his little girl to call him "fat boy," and he indeed was fat and had difficulty losing his extra weight. He was subconsciously convinced that he was a fat person. This can also happen to a woman constantly called an old lady. I use youthful terms in referring to my wife. I want her to take care of herself. Women need rest; they need their beauty sleep. How is a woman who has to work away from home every day going to get sufficient sleep? My wife gets much more rest and sleeps much more than I do. I think all this has kept her appearance youthful and her outlook cheerful. I could choose to focus on negatives in her or things she does wrong as she could in me. Instead I decide to reinforce and praise what is good.

Who can find a woman of worth? Far beyond jewels is her value. Her husband trusts her judgment; he does not lack income. She brings him profit, not loss, all the days of her life. She watches over the affairs of her household, and does not eat the bread of idleness. Her children rise up and call her blessed; her husband, too, praises her: "Many are the women of proven worth, but you have excelled them all." [27]

---

[27] Prov 31: 10-12,27-29

Men are very visually beings as women are emotional. I appreciate the beauty of my wife. I heard a lady say that when woman is loved, she evokes beauty. I have found that to be true. I make sure to give lots of affection and attention to my wife in word and deed. Sometimes it's just emailing her or calling her, and I always make sure to give her some encouragement each time. On a picture of my wife that I posted to my Facebook page a friend commented that she could tell when my wife is cherished by me, her man, because of the peaceful beauty she possesses. It's not the caked up made up photo-shopped cosmetic attraction but the beauty of a woman at peace.

Attraction

While as a gender, men may be more visually stimulated than women are, but it doesn't mean they aren't visually stimulated at all. We all know of girls in their teens and 20's who get boy-crazy and swoon over the "cute" and "buff" athletes and celebrities. Of course they wise up sooner than men because once they bear children, the rearing of them requires a responsible man in the picture, hopefully the one whom she married and who fathered the child. Regardless, they do continue to have attractions of their own. I have spent some time talking above about a man being attracted to his wife, but a wife should also be attracted to her husband. They say to attract, you have to be attractive. So I have made it a practice of keeping myself up so as not to become so "unattractive" to my wife as I age. To do this of course we need to practice the good health habits of exercise and eating right mentioned in Chapter 3. These things take discipline and mastery of the flesh so they are good for the spirit as well as the flesh since we can deny ourselves and enrich our marriages at the same time. I find it a bit humorous at times (and possibly somewhat sad) how young men will work so arduously to attract the attention of young ladies while they are "on the prowl" looking for a mate to marry. Then once they marry they let themselves go and become soft and fat and lazy. I see it as a bit of a "bait and switch." It is as though we are displaying one thing but actually delivering something quite different.

Of course, that's just the beginning. What other things would attract a woman? This may vary from one to the next, but normal women are wired by God to be attracted to masculinity. Maturity and dignity are masculine. Let's consider the masculine things men do that women find attractive. When a man puts on a tool belt and fires up some power tools, it gets a woman's attention—she notices. While women are quite naturally beautiful while at rest, it's not nearly as becoming on a man. There's probably little that women find attractive about men hollering at a television while watching sports or spending endless hours playing video games. Instead, outdoor work that requires "sweat of the brow" (cf Gen 3:19) will get her better grade of attention. Even though we may get dirty and smelly, there is still something about this that attracts a woman. This can actually be a fun thing for a married couple remembering the flirtatious ways they used to work for each other's attention.

Communication

The real way to a woman's heart though is to make an emotional connection, and that is done with communication. Women are very social beings; they care about others. There is really only one way to get to know someone else, and that is by talking with them. True love of course goes way beyond the physical. You have to be in love with the person herself. This requires that we stay connected and keep up with what's going on inside each other. For a Catholic, the marriage is between two people who are composed of body and soul. We should desire to get each other to heaven. So, we need to know what's going on with each other mentally, physically, emotionally, and spiritually. This takes a very broad line of communication. It takes a time commitment.

Communication is going to be a woman's strength, and may be more difficult for men. That means it's going to take some work. We may have to get out of our comfort zone. We may have to commit some time to study on improving our communication skills. It may be that we just need to commit some time to developing the skill with our wives. I know that there can be some emotional things that will weigh a woman down. Realize men, that woman are wired to worry. It is good that God created them in this way as they need to care for babies. But I believe that oftentimes Satan will use this against them or at least against my wife in particular. She will worry about what seems to me to be the strangest things.

It's important for us as men to be able to detect when something is bothering our wives. When we do, we need to get her to talk about it. Women can carry around some heavy emotional baggage, and it can really weigh on them. I know there have been some things over the 24 years of my marriage that I really had to work to get my wife to talk through. But it was all worth the work when she had that release of all that weight lifted off her. She would become free and light-hearted. This can take some courage because we don't always know what it is that is causing the dismay, but we have to use that courage we've been endowed with to rescue our wives from the distress. She is counting on that strength we possess.

We have to make time for communication. As men, we have a lot of responsibilities. If we appear busy, and our wives are sort of aloof or escaping (sometimes called running) from facing something, they will use our busyness as an excuse to let it fester. We can have a cue or a situation established with our wives so that they know we are available for talking. One of the ways my wife and I maintain our closeness, our intimacy, is by spending *lots* of time together alone. Since we have seven children we can easily be distracted from each other. So, we have a committed night together each week when we do just what we want to do. It usually involves a meal together, just the two of us. The ride in the car and dinner are opportune times for communication.

Sometimes though she may not be saying much, and I won't detect that anything is necessarily bothering her. So I'll mention that she's not saying anything. She then normally says "Ask me a question." So I'll think of something to ask her, and that normally will generate a nice meaningful conversation through which our intimacy and knowing of each other can grow. But sometimes she may ask me a question. I don't necessarily mind that she does, but sometimes I may become offended by her questioning. We have come to know each other very well and which buttons we shouldn't press with each other and which ones we should be very delicate with. But there are those things that may worry her needlessly. As I said, Satan will use the gift of concern against her. I tell her she's "listening to the dark voices." I may get a little short or frustrated because it will have been something we've discussed before or a decision I've made based on those discussions. Once I detect this, I realize that it is again an opportunity to explain the considerations given in making the decision and why we are doing what we're doing. It may happen that I have to explain these things several times on occasions, but she is again freed from worry and understands our course.

CHAPTER 12

Leading and Loving

Husbands, love your wives, even as Christ loved the church and handed himself over for her. (Eph 5:25)

The husband is called to be the head of his wife to lead her and protect her so that she can be the feminine woman God created her to be.

You may have noticed that as I outlined the tools and traits we as men naturally possess as given to us by God, I mentioned their importance toward effective leadership. We just need to use these tools we naturally possess for their highest purposes. If we look around we will see men in various leadership roles. This is natural. A small minority of women will try their hand at leadership, but typical femininity plays more of a submissive and assisting role in groups and organizations of all kinds. This is despite the efforts of decades of feminism as they claim to have made great strides in this area. According to St. John Paul II, regardless of the role women are called to play in various facets of society, she should do so in a manner consistent with her feminine nature: "Consequently, even the rightful opposition of women to what is expressed in the biblical words 'He shall rule over you' (*Gen* 3:16) must not under any condition lead to the 'masculinization' of women. In the name of liberation from male 'domination,' women must not appropriate to themselves male characteristics contrary to their own feminine 'originality.'"[28]

As part of a You Tube video series I did in 2012 I had some research done gathering some statistics of female leadership. If we look at some of these, we will see that by default it displays the overwhelming dominance of men in the leadership role in all facets of society. Again, this is AFTER all of the tireless efforts of feminists and their forced affirmative action policies and quotas across the spectrum of societal roles. We looked at leadership statistics in politics which are easily ascertained. Here's where they stood in major political offices in 2012.

Female Political Leaders-2012[29]

Office	#	%
Governors	6	12
US Senators	17	17
US Congresswomen	75	17

In the corporate world, this was their status.

Female Corporate CEO's-2012[30]

Size	#	%
Fortune 500 Companies	18	3.6
Fortune 1,000 Companies	39	3.9

Relatively speaking, most women do not possess the leadership skills men do naturally, and even though they are being offered these positions because of their gender,

---

[28] John Paul II, *Mulieris Dignitatem* ¶10
[29] Wikipedia.org
[30] catalyst.org

many do not want them because the responsibilities clash so severely with their natural femininity. Leadership is a distinctive part of masculinity, plain and simple.

Highest and Best Use

Considering the natural fit we as men have for leadership naturally, we should automatically assume this role in the most important area of our lives, in the family. It is a bit of a mystery as to why so many men who possess such powerful skills of leadership just leave them on the job and return home where their wives are the boss. It just goes to show you the effectiveness and pervasiveness of the feminist ideology in our culture. But we don't need to stop in the natural; we shouldn't even start there. If we start with God's law, based on the teachings of the Church and Holy Scripture, we see that God has ordained that the man be the head of his family. (Eph 5:23) Unfortunately, like with many other contemporary teachings of the Church, this has been confused and misunderstood in the last four to five decades and has severely affected at least two full generations now.

This is where it is so important to understand the teachings of the Church and their structure and character. We should know that our beliefs do not change over time. It doesn't matter what year it is, with regard to faith and morals, the Church's teaching does not change. Of course, the family operates under the moral law of the Church, and she gives us the framework within which to work. From time to time, the Church finds it necessary to reiterate Teaching for the good of the faithful.

> This living transmission, accomplished in the Holy Spirit, is called Tradition, since it is distinct from Sacred Scripture, though closely connected to it. Through Tradition, the Church, in her doctrine, life and worship, perpetuates and transmits to every generation all that she herself is, all that she believes. The sayings of the holy Fathers are a witness to the life-giving presence of this Tradition, showing how its riches are poured out in the practice and life of the Church, in her belief and her prayer. (CCC¶78)

It seems for the most recent centuries, every 75-100 years, or 3 or 4 generations, the Church through the Holy Father, has issued official documents that reaffirm her consistent Teachings. The important thing to keep in mind here is that this teaching does not change. So, while some wording or emphasis may vary from one document to another, any new documents should be read in terms of the previous with regard to principle. We may gain a deeper understanding of a Truth in time, but never would have a new belief that would contradict a basic Truth.

In dealing with the issue of leadership or order in the family, the specific types of Papal Documents we want to consider now are Encyclical Letters, Apostolic Letters, and Apostolic Exhortations. Essentially, these types of documents have a hierarchical order to authority. Encyclical Letters are second in authority only to Apostolic Constitution giving instruction on doctrine. These are followed by Apostolic Letters and Apostolic Exhortations which do not instruct in doctrine.[31]

So when we see an encyclical letter come out, we need to pay particular attention because it carries the weight of the Pope's teaching authority. One of the more controversial encyclicals in recent history was Humanae Vitae which upheld the Church's prohibition of the use of artificial contraception.

So pertinent to our issue here of family hierarchy, if we want this level of teaching we have to go back to 1930 to a document called Casti Connubbi from Pope Pius XI. In this encyclical letter, the Holy Father upholds the long standing teaching of the Church that that husband is the head of the family.

> Domestic society being confirmed, therefore, by this bond of love, there should flourish in it that 'order of love,' as St. Augustine calls it. This order includes both the primacy of the husband with regard to the wife and children, the ready subjection of the wife and her willing obedience. For if the man is the head, the woman is the heart, and as he occupies the chief place in ruling, so she may and ought to claim for herself the chief place in love."[32]

This instruction is beautifully plain and easy to understand. The symbolism of the head and the heart add to both the simplicity and beauty, and any of us who

---

[31] www.law.edu "Church Documents Overview"

[32] Pius XI , *Casti Connubbi* (Encyclical Letter on Christian Marriage) ¶26-27, accessed September 1, 2015, http://w2.vatican.va/content/pius-xi/en/encyclicals.index.html

are married can relate to how this would apply to us in marriage. We can witness and attest that through the centuries and generations how this wonderful order has served families and thereby society so well. However, in recent years, many seem to believe that we have become "wiser" and more civilized as to think we can change this order instituted by God. Some of the more progressives and liberals who are not willing to uphold traditional teaching can take things out of context and assume that new doctrine can be created. A case in point would be St. John Paul II's Apostolic Letter "Mulieris Dignitatem," or "On the Dignity and Vocation of Women." In this letter, the Holy Father beautifully and accurately states "… the awareness that in marriage there is mutual 'subjection of the spouses out of reverence for Christ', and not just that of the wife to the husband, must gradually establish itself in hearts, consciences, behavior and customs." (¶24) Does this mean that the Holy Father could be altering the Church's teaching in this area? Obviously, that is simply not possible. So what is it that he's saying here?

He is quoting the Scriptures which are also consistent within themselves. Why would St. Paul say for wives to be submissive to their husbands in one breath, but for husbands and wives to submit to one another in another if one command cancelled out the other? Obviously the two passages are referring to two different things. The Holy Father is saying that there isn't "JUST" a submission of the wife to the husband alone. In his words he explains it as such in the previous sentence to the above quote "This is especially true because the husband is called the 'head' of the wife as Christ is the head of the Church; he is so in order to give 'himself up for her' (Eph 5:25), and giving himself up for her means giving up even his own life." He acknowledges that the husband is the "head" and clarifies the type of headship he should administer. It must always be considered in respect to the mutual respect that they have for each other. With that being said, still one person has to lead the family, and as evidenced by the quotation from Pius XI above, that person is the husband. We have a beautiful continuity in our Church's teaching.

However, so often today men do not take on this leadership role. Most are not taught this, and many were brought up either with their mothers leading over their fathers or with no father in the home at all. So, what is a wife to do then? Pope Pius XI answers that in Casti Connubbi: "Again, this subjection of wife to husband in its degree and manner may vary according to the different conditions of persons, place and time. In fact, if the husband neglect his duty, it falls to the wife to take his place in directing."[33] Notice that there is a very distinct qualifier there. "If" he neglects his duty, then the wife must lead. So, she does not automatically lead or even share in the leadership at the outset as many claim is the innovation today. It is only if he fails in his duty. This means he has that right and duty at the outset. It is his to lose by default because of the role given to him by God. Also, notice he actually softens the term. Previously he said the husband has a place in "ruling,"

---

[33]Pius XI , *Casti Connubbi* (Encyclical Letter on Christian Marriage) ¶28, accessed September 1, 2015, http://w2.vatican.va/content/pius-xi/en/encyclicals.index.html

but with regard to the wife, she should take his place in "directing." But understand that when this happens, it is compromised. It should not be the norm or an "option." When something is compromised, it is not as is intended, so it will be lacking in some way and to some extent; it will be weaker than the ideal. So, a good Catholic should do everything possible to order things as God has intended.

Love as Christ Loves

St. John Paul II above emphasizes the type of head the husband is supposed to be by quoting St. Paul in Scripture, that we husbands are to love our wives as Christ loves the Church. How does Christ love? Does He turn over His leadership role to the Church? Obviously not. He led in an unselfish way, sacrificing and giving the ultimate gift of His very Life. We are to do the same as husbands. We are not to use our leadership role for our own selfish desires. This is actually how many men shirk their leadership role. They are so wrapped up in their own pleasures that they have no capacity to lead. Leadership is work; it is not something that can be done passively. We must be attentive; we have to be interested.

Let's look at how we lead in other capacities. We are proactive. We have a plan. We have goals. We go to work on that plan to reach those goals. This is how we are to lead a family. We should have a bit of a "blueprint" for our family, albeit somewhat of a "fluid" blueprint. As a husband and wife get started on their family together, they will have some dreams and aspirations. Obviously this is not all about the husband. As a leader, we consider all involved in the group we are leading.   So first and foremost, for a newly married couple, the husband needs to be concerned for the well-being of his bride. The way I have always stated it was that I found when I got married that my top priority was to make sure my wife was happy. That may sound a bit misleading as though I would take her lead until I explain what I mean. As the stronger member of the couple, I am to be my wife's protector. So, I am looking out for her. When I say I ensure her happiness, it doesn't mean that she always gets what she wants as though she were a spoiled child. Most of the time she does and has because we are on the same page with things, have open communication, and understand how we are going to accomplish things through our discussions.   But sometimes she may want something or want to do something, but I will bring up an issue or concern that she may not have considered. I will discuss it with her and explain why it would not be good for her to do or have that particular desired thing. In such case, I may could consider or ask of any possible way to overcome that concern, or I may have a strong enough reason to deny that she go that route. By rule of her requirement to be submissive, she is obliged to follow my directive. Ultimately, she will be happy for having obeyed God by following me and for my loving concern for her.

So, when a couple is newly married, their passion for each other should be at an all time high. They would long to express that love physically, but have had to wait until they are married to share themselves completely with each other. The normal result of this is conjugal union is the conception of a child, a true blessing from God. Sometimes couples may have the inability to conceive, and this is truly difficult for them. "Couples who discover that they are sterile suffer greatly. 'What will you give me,' asks Abraham of God, 'for I continue childless?' And Rachel cries to her husband Jacob, 'Give me children, or I shall die!'"(CCC¶2374) The attitude of a Catholic couple should be to see children as a blessing and to desire them in their marriage from the outset based on the perspective of the Church of requiring that all acts of sexuality be open to life. "Fecundity is a gift, an end of marriage, for conjugal love naturally tends to be fruitful. A child does not come from outside as something added on to the mutual love of the spouses, but springs from the very heart of that mutual giving, as its fruit and fulfillment. So the Church, which is 'on the side of life,' teaches that 'it is necessary that each and every marriage act remain ordered per se to the procreation of human life.' 'This particular doctrine, expounded on numerous occasions by the Magisterium, is based on the inseparable connection, established by God, which man on his own initiative may not break, between the unitive significance and the procreative significance which are both inherent to the marriage act.'"(CCC¶2366)

While the Church prohibits the use of artificial contraception under this doctrine, a couple may use periodic abstinence when there is a serious (just) reason for postponing a conception. In this case all marital acts are still open to conception as required by Church law, but the likelihood of a conception is severely limited. For this reason, the circumstances must justify the practice of abstinence in this way. It would be difficult to imagine that it would be the norm for all couples to enter into marriage where such circumstances exist. However, it is highly likely and almost probable that a young couple would have a relatively low income, or one not as high as they had grown accustomed to with their parents. So, the concept of "just starting out" would probably not be sufficient reason to deliberately postpone a conception. If that were the case, the couple should just likely postpone getting married until they are financially ready to have children. As presented in Chapter 2, the prospective groom should be along in his career well enough to support himself and a family before marrying.

So, a newly married couple should put their faith and trust in God as they embark on their new adventure of marriage. They should naturally physically love each as a passionate newly married couple would in the Garden of Eden with the hope that they will conceive a child. A Catholic man should want to give his wife children. This is what a woman naturally wants in marriage. Then she should be allowed to stay home and raise the children. She should be allowed to bear her new baby naturally and to focus her complete attention on the little one she has carried beneath her heart for the last nine months who has squirmed around inside her and grown accustomed to hearing her sweet voice. She should be allowed to bond with him and hold him securely without a time limit. The cold "maternity leave" period that is imposed by an employer has no place in the life of a Catholic family. A child deserves to be raised by his mother, not some stranger at a daycare center. The mother and the child deserve this to be provided by the man of the family. This is what it means for a man to give his life. This is what it means for a man to love his wife as Christ loves the Church. They will likely have to sacrifice. They will likely have to do without luxuries and some of the extras to which they grew accustomed with their parents. They will get to know what love really is beyond the consumerism of society. They will get to appreciate and focus on the gift of life that has come from the love they share as a couple as they experience the awesome and wondrous participation with God in creation.

> Parents have the first responsibility for the education of their children. They bear witness to this responsibility first by creating a home where tenderness, forgiveness, respect, fidelity, and disinterested service are the rule. The home is well suited for education in the virtues. This requires an apprenticeship in self-denial, sound judgment, and self-mastery - the preconditions of all true freedom. Parents should teach their children to subordinate the "material and instinctual dimensions to interior and spiritual ones." Parents have a grave responsibility to give good example to their children.(CCC¶2223)

Safeguarding the mother and child setting

A woman is very vulnerable at the time of a pregnancy. She will lean on and cling to her husband very particularly during this time. She will be weak; she will get tired. As I once heard it said by a mother with a child in her womb "It's hard work making a baby." What could be truer? The baby is the ultimate of vulnerability once he is born. He is dependent for everything, most of which should come from his mother. God made this design for creation, and it is for this reason a family is necessary for the bearing of children and the continuation of humanity. A strong man is required in a family to protect the weak and vulnerable. The husband is careful to protect his wife and children from the harshness of the world.

Their home is like a haven, a quiet safe place for the mother and child to bond together. How can a man send his young wife out of the house before daybreak with an infant to drop him off with a stranger while she tries to work all day long thinking of her baby? The two should be at home together where the child can develop naturally in his home with his mother, not in a group center with a multitude of other babies. A baby deserves the loving attention and affection of his mother. A mother deserves the opportunity to watch her child grow without the looming date of her separation from him, watching the calendar and callusing her heart for the impending separation. She should be the one to hear his first word and to see him take his first steps. How much of a child's life does his mother miss because she is separated from him!

It is for these reasons that we can suspect is the cause of the very low birthrate in our society. How many women are not allowed to be true to themselves, to their true feminine motherly nature? When a woman has to subdue her feelings of longing for her child again and again on a constant daily basis, she grows cold and manly. When she has to miss out on the events of her child's life over and over, a little part of her dies inside each time. She can only take so much of this, so she will sterilize herself or get her husband to sterilize himself. This is the tragic end to so many marriages. Currently the divorce rate is roughly 50%, and economist Robert

Michael attributed "an enormous amount of the increase in the divorce rate to contraceptives."[34]

As Catholic men, for those of us who marry, we are to maintain and safeguard the mother and child setting of the home. This should be the impetus and orientation of our work, our homes, and our very lives. This takes on much greater meaning than the worldly selfishness of the ultimate end of satisfying one's pleasures. When we have a focus of creating a setting where a family can be allowed to take root and flourish, we approach life in a much different way and realize the great calling God has for us. This is the real call of Catholic manhood today, if we are only willing to reorient ourselves and become obedient.

---

[34] Dr. Janet E. Smith "Contraception: Why Not" (Federal Way, WA: Trinity Formation Resources, 2004) (audio CD)

CHAPTER 13

Fathering

The just walk in integrity;
happy are their children after them!(Prov. 20:7)

Fathering is the logical outgrowth of a loving and successful marriage in that love grows and produces life.

Next to being the husband and intimate companion to a very happy and loving wife, fathering would be the topic I could speak most to after having been working at it for the last 22 years. Of course I don't mean fathering merely in the sense of conceiving children with my wife, but actually being a father to them. We've all heard the expression "Any man could be a father but it takes a real man to be a dad." As of this writing, our "baby" is 6 years old, but before his birth we had only a gap of 4 years between babies, we had a fairly steady routine of welcoming a new little person into the world every couple of years or so. But of course that's only the beginning, because we are all aware of the amount of commitment a child requires. It's not like a pet or a house even, a child is eternal. So once you have them, you have them for life.

Being a Dad

I once heard a man say after splitting up with his wife that he knew he wasn't meant to remain single because he loved kids so much. Someone who might observe me, might think that I really like kids. I could say I do to an extent, but if someone strictly liked kids, I would say they should work at a daycare or teach elementary school. That should satisfy that desire. Educational consultant Jim Stenson says "We are not here to raise kids; we are here to raise adults." That pretty much sums up the way I've always seen being a dad. I can't say that I was really comfortable with the concept of having babies, or having my wife have babies, you know. I wasn't so familiar with babies at all. I was the baby in my family, and it wasn't until several years before I got married that my sister had started a family. That would have been my first experience with infants. Don't get me wrong, I absolutely loved it, and now I have a hard time believing that I miss having babies around. They were a great deal of work, and I'm sure I just miss the idea of it, but God knows what He's doing. When you're at the childbearing age, you have what it takes to be a dad, over and over.

Just the process from conception to the baby growing in his mommy's womb and watching the changes a woman goes through during pregnancy are all completely fascinating to me. It was something that never really got old. There's a special kind of bonding that goes on during pregnancy between mother, child, and father. A child hears his mother's voice all day long while in her womb, but he also hears his dad's voice when he is present. He knows his dad's voice from the beginning of his life. You probably know that everyone has a unique voice, like a fingerprint. Every child will always know their dad's voice for life, if he is a committed dad.

I was present for the natural births of all of my 7 children. It was an amazing experience each time. To be there to see another child enter the world, to see my child, enter the world is difficult to put to words. Each child was so perfectly made and healthy, all gifts from God. That's really all a man could want out of life. To behold this tiny vulnerable little person who's totally dependent upon his mother primarily for all the necessities of life, but also indirectly dependent on his dad. He's so vulnerable, but yet completely self-contained. All of his biological processes are intact, and he doesn't need any supplementary devices to make him operate or keep him going. Pretty soon he will also be able to locomote. I'm sure you're thinking that even an animal is capable of all that—exactly. And that's the next thought. This little being has a mind of his own. Right, and not only that, he also has a soul. This little being is eternal. What a grave responsibility we as dads have. Yes, we are the heads of our families, and with that role comes the ultimate of responsibilities.

So, yes a man fathers children by producing the seed to impregnate his wife, and an immortal person enters the world. That man has undertaken an awesome responsibility. When a person is "in charge" he is the one who is responsible. So yes, he is the head of his family, and his wife is to submit to his headship, but that does not mean that he is to take advantage of his position for his own pleasures and comfort. Remember St. Paul says to "love your wife even as Christ loved the Church and handed himself over for her."(Eph 5:25) So this means the headship is one of service and sacrifice. A wife is submissive to her husband because she is ultimately submitting to God. This is the order of love St. Augustine speaks of. [35] When she is submissive and

---

[35] Pius XI , *Casti Connubbi* (Encyclical Letter on Christian Marriage) ¶26, accessed September 1, 2015,

respectful to her husband she is setting an example to her children. She is also setting an example to them when she does not respect or submit to him. A man should be astute to point this out to his wife when necessary. By obeying her husband, a wife is assisting her children in being obedient and making things easier on herself in the long run.

A man can also make it easier on his wife for her to respect him by being respectable. The principal way we can attain respect is by conducting ourselves with a manner of dignity. The appearance of dignity is an all-encompassing very far-reaching concept. It involves the way we act, how we dress, how we speak, and what we do. It is helpful to remember that children learn from what they see. They are not very good with listening to lecturing or a set of rules and following them, especially the very young ones. They are very good at emulating what they see. They follow example. So, if a man dresses in a sloppy manner, his child will dress the same. If he dresses with some dignity, the child will as well.

The men with whom I associate are very cautious about mode of attire for Holy Mass. Most of these men will wear a suit or coat and tie to Mass on Sunday. It is no surprise that their sons do so as well. The natural response to that observation is that the parents dressed the child, and that is true. But I as well as all of these dads had the experience that their sons wanted to dress up the way their dads did. This is the essence of "being a dad." I mentioned earlier that I am a

http://w2.vatican.va/content/pius-xi/en/encyclicals.index.html

runner and enjoy the sport. All five of my sons wanted to run when they were old enough. Our kids want to be just like us. Our sons want to be like us, and our daughters will be attracted to men like us. Please read that statement again, particularly with regard to our daughters. I have seen so many young ladies marry men who were just like their fathers, despite their severe lack of dignity or, better described, severely slothful nature.

We need to consider how we conduct ourselves in a general manner. Are we serious or are we silly? Silliness in a man is a terrible sight to behold. You can see why it would be so difficult for a woman to respect a silly man. "Sin creates a proclivity to sin; it engenders vice by repetition of the same acts. This results in perverse inclinations which cloud conscience and corrupt the concrete judgment of good and evil. Thus sin tends to reproduce itself and reinforce itself, but it cannot destroy the moral sense at its root."(CCC¶1865) He may have been the life of the party during their dating days, but once you marry and have children, a different kind of man is needed, a real one. "The tongue of the wise pours out knowledge, but the mouth of fools spews folly."(Proverbs 15:2) This doesn't mean that a man must always be stern and distant. I know people who never had any level of interaction with their dads as kids, or very little. A dad can be involved and engaged with their children even at a young age without acting silly. It's actually a very gratifying and admirable thing to see a mature man interacting in a dignified even playful manner with his young child. He can do this without being childish or silly, and it is actually heart-warming. This is the manifestation of true joy that should be part of the spirit of a Catholic.

I've always stayed engaged with my kids through sports. When we are all younger, including myself, and still some now, we enjoyed playing baseball together. This gave me an opportunity to teach them something physical, something outside of books. I know this may not be practical for all men, but that's the way I chose to do it. It may be something different for other dads like fishing, hunting, or camping. I think it's important to be genuine and to find a genuine connection with your own kids. That's what comes across to them. They can detect when our heart is into something and not. It will come across in our attitude if we really enjoy what we're doing. It is a way to pass something on that we possess and that we receive. As we have all matured, we may not play together as much but have drifted more into spectating together. Again, it is a connection; something light we can discuss recreationally. Actually on that note, watching sports had become a distraction from the kids when they were little. So, I actually got away from it completely for a while. When they started having an appreciation and an interest in following sports, I joined in. You can see how this works. We adjust ourselves to be able to stay connected to our kids.

This isn't to say that we can't learn new things together as well. One of the greatest institutions in America is the family business. Entrepreneurship is the grid this country was built upon. Obviously it started with agriculture where you had the family farm, and the kids were naturally given responsibilities on the farm. There still a little bit of farming going on today, but most of it has been industrialized and automated as the rest of the economy has. This isn't necessarily something to lament as a forlorn nostalgic loss. Being true to myself,

I would have been miserable on a farm. I'm just not into that. I do office work. But I did get outside my comfort zone to learn a little bit about real estate and was able to get the kids involved while learning. We slowly got into it mostly acquiring a lot at a time and hiring out labor to build the houses. The kids were still pretty young, 10 and under, so we'd just go out together and cut the lot on weekends, and when the construction started we'd monitor the progress each day or several times during the week after I'd get off of work. We would consider and plan to get them more into the actual construction when they got older. Some of that did happen, but I was never really able to juggle it with my job to learn it with them. So those that were interested learned at least some from others in the craft, but I have stayed involved from the outside. My personal participation is in the investment side, and I will continue to coach up my kids in that segment. But the point is, it has been something we've journeyed through together. It's important that they see us engaged in dignified things when at work and at recreation. It doesn't send a very good message to a child to see their dad tied up in a video game while he is ignoring his family.

Finally on this topic, let's consider how we speak. As far as our choice of words, we need to avoid regular and frequent use of slang. It is important as the primary educators of our children that we set an example of proper speech. This doesn't mean that we need to be excessively formal or speak over their heads beyond what they can understand, but can speak in clear distinct terms for them to learn proper speech. We should not speak in childish terms either. We also need to take care in our tone and attitude in speaking. I have heard dads speak in a very demeaning or insulting way. I have also heard some who are overly critical of others or portray themselves as know-it-alls. We should speak with a charitable tone, but also directly without being whiny or feminine. We should speak in a way that portrays a humble confidence that will inspire the trust and respect of those in our family.

This may take some practice because often we will find in a family setting that the mother is doing much of the talking especially in directing things around the house and coordinating activities of the children. As the head of the family, the father should have his interest their first. As a way to invoke this, the father could initiate discussion, especially at meals, asking of the kids activities of the day and their plans for the days ahead. If he initiates and inquires, the mother who will often be the one who is more hands-one with them will be in the natural responsive position in these discussions. Other ways to practice this more may be for the father to do some sort of reading or teaching to the family. It may be reading from Scripture, some religious study together like reading the Saint of the day at the breakfast table, or vocal prayer like recitation of the Rosary. All of these require that we verbalize ourselves. When doing so, we should pay attention to how we sound. I have heard of some so bold as to record themselves to really know how they sound. If you try it, it may shock you. Regardless, if we listen to radio or television commentators or orators of any sort we will notice how differently they will speak that the average person and the amount of respect and confidence it commands.

Child Training and Discipline

The father of the family should be the primary disciplinarian of the children. There are varying views today about the ideal methods of discipline. From a Catholic viewpoint, I would say Dr. Ray Guarendi has a well-balanced approach to discipline of children. There must be an establishment of obedience that is expected by the children based on respect for the parents. As mentioned above, the wife can set a good example of obedience and respect in the way she responds to her husband. She should display a loving respect for her husband in an air of desire to please him.

The father with the input of his wife and based upon their understanding of the most effective methods of discipline will lay down some rules for their home and children, things they will be allowed to do and not which can and will change based on age and maturity. Some things obviously may never be allowed, but others may change. There does not necessarily need to be a specific age that every child will be allowed to do certain things. This can vary depending on the child and circumstances. The important thing is that each child knows at present what is allowed and what is not and that they be expected to obey. If and when they do not obey, there should be just consequences based upon those methods of discipline researched. Based on the decision of the father of the level of standards of behavior (again with the input of his wife, but as his ultimate decision), that same level of discipline and standard should be enforced by his wife when he is not present. When he is present, he should be the one enforcing the level of standards and discipline and not rely on his wife to do it. In this way, he is the primary disciplinarian. She is secondary in his absence but is showing subjection and respect to him by enforcing his rule.

As dads, we are not there to be our children's friend. We are there to raise these children into adults. We are tasked with the responsibility of the formation of these children by training them in the home. We should train our children from a very young age. Even as toddlers, we can set up training sessions where we tell them to do something and observe as they obey the command. We must have the expectation that they will obey the first time. It can be a fun learning experience between father and child as they learn to be respectful and obedient to authority. We shouldn't just go haphazardly throughout each day waiting for them to do something unacceptable and then correct them for it without them knowing they've done something wrong. This is unfair to the child. For a dad to do this training, he has to take time away from his personal or business interests and focus on his children. In this way we are forming obedient children respectful to authority from a very young age that will carry on into adolescence and adulthood.

Throughout this whole process of their young tender lives and into childhood and teenage years it is critical that the mother back up and enforce her husband's rule showing the utmost respect for him. Again as stated, this is not to overinflate her husband or to deify him, but to set an example and to submit herself to God in her role as a wife and mother. It is also not to place herself on a lower level of dignity than her husband. God created us all with equal dignity. "Man and woman have been created, which is to say, willed by God: on the one hand, in perfect equality as human persons; on the other, in their respective beings as man and woman. 'Being man' or 'being woman' is a reality which is good and willed by God: man and woman possess an inalienable dignity which comes to them immediately from God their Creator. Man and woman are both with one and the same dignity 'in the image of God'. In their 'being-man' and 'being-woman', they reflect the Creator's wisdom and goodness."(CCC¶369) Children also have dignity but yet another role in the family separate from and subject to their parents. Eventually children will enter adolescence and the teenage years and begin to naturally test the limits of discipline, as they start to move in a direction of independence. This is a healthy expression of their development, but they still need to feel that those limits are enforced. If the order above is not followed, what typically happens is that the children will test the limits and their mother will sympathize and side with them against their father instead of being faithful to her husband. This is due to the emotional process she is going through watching her children grow. She has to entrust her children to their father's guidance. If she does not, the children will play their mother against their father in order to get their way. Ultimately, it could mean the end of the marriage as the children rebel and get into trouble, sometimes ruining their entire lives. We likely all can think of an instance with someone we know had this happen in their family. If we look at the situation, it is likely that this order was not followed.

Spiritual Headship

A critical dimension of fathering we need to take up is the spiritual leadership in our families. However, in many Catholic Churches today we will often experience an excessive expression of femininity in the Mass and in other forms of prayer as well as in the leading of activities in the Church even though we are led exclusively by a male Priesthood. We as fathers need to still lead spiritually in our families even when the male leadership may be lacking in the Church. The guidelines for Faith in Chapter 8 are an excellent framework to insert into the spiritual life of a family. We have to start by knowing the basics of Church teaching, the basic dogma or beliefs that we accept. Then we need to know the precepts or requirements for practicing our faith, like attendance of Mass on Sundays and Holy Days. We have to lead our family in obedience to these precepts understanding the requirements under the pain of sin. Then we need to be able to pass the Faith on my teaching them and praying together as a family.

It is important for us to know the theology of our Faith as in the beliefs about the Real Presence of Jesus in the Blessed Sacrament, the role of the Blessed Virgin Mary, the authority of the Pope, etc. Just as important though is that we know and understand the moral law of the Church that pertains to things such as contraception, abortion, marriage, and sexuality. We need to lead our families from this perspective as we set the standards of behavior for our wives and children. Knowing the moral law of the Church, we need to set standards and limits for dress, especially that of our daughters, and when it is appropriate for dating to begin, etc. This will also guide us on what things we should allow pertaining to entertainment including television, use of the internet, music, and video games. There are many things in the media which are below the grade of Catholic morality from which we should protect our children. If we don't use the Catholic moral law as our guide, we have no moral compass so we'll end up allowing whatever is done by those around us and what is seen in the media.

A proper practice of the Faith is an excellent teaching tool. In fact, it is the most effective. It is very damaging to the Faith of children to try to learn something so intangible from a textbook and then to see the exact opposite take place in their Catholic schools, Churches, and yes even in their very own home with Catholic parents. I am convinced that this is precisely the reason for the exodus from the Church by so many young people raised in Catholic households and educated in ostensibly Catholic schools. Theologically, the unique Gift present in the Catholic Church is the Blessed Sacrament. We are charged as fathers with ensuring that the belief in the Real Presence of Jesus in the Holy Eucharist is instilled in our children. It should of course be verbally communicated to them. But they also need to learn it in practice. There is a saying that if you don't act as though you believe, you will begin to believe the way you act, attributed to Venerable Fulton J. Sheen. We need to act as though God is really present when we are in a Catholic Church or otherwise in the Presence of the Blessed Sacrament, because we are. We should not act casually or chat with our neighbor or family, and we should dress like we are in the presence of a King, because we are. For instance, when we go into Church, we should not walk in the way we would walk into a movie theater in a clustered group chatting and giggling as we take our seats and wait for the show. We should walk in silently and respectfully in a deliberate spirit of reverence genuflecting before entering the pew and kneeling to pray having come into the Presence of God. We should receive Holy Communion on the tongue while kneeling and instruct our children on doing the same, never touching the Host. This is our right in the Church. While the disciplines of the Church also allow for the reception of Communion in the hand while standing,[36] it is important that we consider the stipulations and why. When Communion in the hand was first allowed, it had to be done so with an indult (or permission) for the "exception" to the norm of the Church.

> Where a contrary usage, that of placing holy communion on the hand, prevails, the Holy See—wishing to help them fulfill their task, often difficult as it is nowadays—lays on those conferences the task of weighing carefully whatever special circumstances may exist there, taking care to avoid any risk of lack of respect or of false opinions with regard to the Blessed Eucharist, and to avoid any other ill effects that may follow.[37]

---

[36] Francis Cardinal Arinze, *Redemptionis Sacramentum* (On Certain matters to be observed or avoided regarding the Most Holy Eucharist) No. 92, accessed September 2, 2015, http://www.vatican.va/roman_curia/congregations/ccdds/index.htm

[37] MEMORIALE DOMINI, Instruction on the Manner of Distributing Holy Communion, Sacred Congregation for Divine

Notice the caution and concern there was amongst the Congregation at the Vatican and the Holy Father for allowing such an variation and the severe dangers that were feared. With regard to standing versus kneeling, Redemptionis Sacramentum states "However, if they receive Communion standing, it is recommended that they give due reverence before the reception of the Sacrament, as set forth in the same norms."[38] The point being here that we as fathers are working to instill belief in the Real Presence to our children (as well as preserve it in ourselves). It is recommended here to follow the age-old tradition of the Church so the concerns mentioned herein can be avoided and we have the best chance for preservation of the Faith. This is a right we have as the faithful that cannot be denied by any Priest; the option to receive on the tongue kneeling is *always* allowed *everywhere*. No dispensation is needed as with the other method. We as fathers are charged with training and teaching our children, (CCC¶2223, 2225) so we have the right to instruct our children in this practice as well.

We need to take care to take our family to a Church where there is a Holy Reverence observed in Church. For our family, we always sought the Church where the most reverence was observed even if we had to inconveniently travel a bit of a distance. This sends a

Worship, May 29, 1969 accessed September 2, 2015, https://www.ewtn.com/library/CURIA
[38] Francis Cardinal Arinze, *Redemptionis Sacramentum* (On Certain matters to be observed or avoided regarding the Most Holy Eucharist) No. 90, accessed September 2, 2015, http://www.vatican.va/roman_curia/congregations/ccdds/index.htm

powerful message to our children, and we communicate to them our reason for doing this. We want to make sure the belief in the Real Presence is deeply instilled in them as this is the most important belief in the Catholic Faith.

Our practice of the Faith and our piety should be moderate and fit the family. Sometimes it may not be a good thing for the mother or the father to go to daily Mass. If the children are not well disciplined and the father is needed at home, he possibly should not be in Mass every day. He is needed at home with his family. Some weekday Masses are good. We have found that at least one during the week helps to sustain us as a family as we all attend together. At this point I have found that attending twice during the week is helpful to me while still being home enough on other days. Adoration is another form of sustenance. It is primary for the head of the family and again should be done around family time. Early on and still to this day, I would go to make Holy Hours of Adoration after the family has gone to bed. At other times I have gone somewhat earlier and started taking the children when they were around 7 years old and preparing for their First Communion. They wanted to emulate their dad.

A good habit to form is the daily recitation of the Holy Rosary with the family with the father leading this and nighttime prayer before bed. It is the ideal way to round out the day. It is also ideal time for training young children on how to behave in Mass. So I would always hold the baby or toddler during our Rosary every evening on my lap.

All these things mentioned are led by the father and his masculine approach is naturally observed by the children. They grow up seeing that religion is not something just for the girls. If the father is not active in the Faith, then the children, especially the boys will see Church as something feminine or sissy. With the father leading, all the children will see the proper order of the father standing in the place of God in his family and will learn obedience and reverence in the practice of the Faith.

Chapter 14

Guiding

Hear, O children, a father's instruction, be attentive,
that you may gain understanding!(Prov. 4:1)

Fathers are to prepare their children for adulthood and guide them through the transition toward independence.

Guiding is the period of our fatherhood when we get to see the results of our labors of approximately 20 years with each child. This is the time where we release our children into the world of independence. It is the time when we find out how well we've done at preparing our children for their entrance into adulthood, when they go out into the world. My goal has always been to raise my children myself and train them to be disciplined and strong, to become leaders, and to go into a troubled world and make it better. As I write this, I have 3 adult children, none of whom are completely independent. One is 23, another is 20, and the other is 18. This is a very tricky and sometimes volatile period in a person's life. It is also a bit tricky for the parents. For their whole lives, our children have been dependent on us for everything. Suddenly, they believe they have complete independence, or act like it anyway. This is actually a good thing if done within reason. As mentioned before, we're here to raise adults. So we don't want them to be dependent on us forever; they can't be. We parents are going to die after all, so they'll eventually need to be able to get on without us.

Letting Go Slowly

The tricky part for parents is that we typically can't or won't just eject them from the house on their 18th birthday. There is a transition period where more and more liberties are allowed, but we still keep a close pulse on how they are handling the adjustment. That's why it's called guiding. In order to do this, we'll have to have had a close relationship with them in earlier years. We will have to have been involved in their day-to-day lives knowing the details of their involvements and relationships. Still, even if we have they will suddenly seem to become more distant and quiet. They are working on trying to figure things out themselves and trying to figure themselves out. They want to know how they fit in to this big puzzle of the world. Up until now, it's all been pretty much academic, literally. They really haven't had to genuinely consider getting serious about life. The responsibilities they've had have been within the context of the shelter of a home. Now they have to start thinking of eventually a home of their own where their parents don't live. We may each remember that experience. For some of us it's more recent than for others.

For us, this process may have been more pronounced than for others. Missy and I have been relatively slow with allowing our children liberties. Personally, I think children today are forced to "grow up" too young. Most aren't really growing up. They are just forced into some unsupervised and indulged situations that expose them to things at much too early of an age, in my opinion. The solution to that for us has been to wait until some of these liberties were necessary. Homeschooling has helped this slow-down process immensely. Also, we exercised reasonable moderation in activities away from home at the same time. This cut down on the need for cell phones at a young age. They didn't need them because they were always with us. We were also able to delay them driving because they didn't have to be away from home as much.

As they have grown and matured, at the point it has become necessary and practical some of these liberties have been added. When they are granted, the kids feel that sense of independence but at a more mature age. Regardless, they still feel like they are making progress and experiencing more freedom. But we as parents have to stay connected and monitor how they are handling this newfound freedom. We have to check their behavior against the standards from which they were formed. How closely are they sticking to them? Which ones are they relaxing and why? We've all heard that each child is different, and that is obviously true. Their personality differences will cause them to set standards possibly different from the ones on which they were raised. In all likelihood, they will relax on some standards, or what we'd call lower their standards. This is often referred to as rebellion. They will all do it in some way or another. The key is to assure that it is not done in a sinful manner.

So, we see the "letting go" process isn't one of just kicking them out of the nest to suddenly fend for themselves. It is a transition process where we walk beside them. Oftentimes, we'll have to walk at a distance, but we still walk. They need the opportunity to do things themselves, to learn the ropes about the real work, to take on real-life responsibilities.

The Guiding Process

I think when we get to the stage of dealing with adult children it is important to really try to remember what it was like to be their age. We should try to remember what we were going through, what we knew, what we didn't know, our attitudes, our likes and dislikes, the things that occupied our thoughts, and the things we desired most. This can be a challenge, but I have found that it is helpful. I have made a practice of thinking back to my first job, my first car, my graduating from high school, and entering college. This has been an immense help in working to relate to my older children and the things they are encountering at this crucial stage in their lives.

But it doesn't stop with this nostalgia or reminiscing. We then have to combine or meld those memories with the experience and wisdom we've gained from just living life as an adult. What were the important choices we made and subsequent things we did that got us from there to today? What mistakes did we make that we wish we wouldn't have made. We'll want to guard our kids against making the same mistakes. Obviously, if there were errors or bad choices that had a tragic impact, then we'd want to do everything the stop our children from repeating them. But others they may have to repeat, hopefully to a lesser extent, in order to learn the associated lessons. We've all heard of learning the hard way, and we've all done some of it, some more than others.

One of these particular areas involves the management of money and the related activities. They should start handling some money and using a bank account as adults. They need to learn the habit of saving and staying within their means. Many parents never make this transition with their kids. They just give them a credit card and pay for everything. At some point, they need to learn the responsibility of money management, and often that point is later than it should have been. Like with anything new, the amounts should be small. They need to have a job or be able to earn money in some way. I mention that Catholic women who will marry should not be career-driven. But they still can find ways to earn a little bit of spending money. My adult daughter does some work for me in my practice that does not put her in contact with my clients. She also teaches piano lessons on a small scale and helps out with some domestic and child care duties for ladies in two separate households. This gives her some responsibilities without tying her down to a full-time job.

But they can take that small income they earn and learn to budget it and direct it to where they want it to go. They need to be able to spend it as they would like. It's theirs after all. But they also need to learn the value of things. When they have to pay for something they want as opposed to need, they have to think twice about actually getting it. They even more so need to learn the value of things they need like food, shelter, and clothing. My older children have been buying their own clothes for a while now. They also will share in the cost of their meals. Depending on the situation, I may even charge them rent for living at home. It's a learning process of not feeling entitled to things but having to put forth effort or money for them. I may not monitor each of their bank accounts, but I watch what they are doing and ask about things and remind them of things so they don't get themselves into trouble.

My oldest son started out working in construction in his high school years and continued after graduating. He even built himself an investment property and still has it today. That's not bad for a 23-year-old. If I were to put that in terms of myself as I mentioned above about putting myself in his place, my main goal in life when I got married was to eventually own a home of my own for my family to live in. I realized that goal at age 26. It was a bit of an anti-climatic event; what would I shoot for next? Nevertheless, contrast that with a young man who built an investment property at 21 years of age. But I've had to stay plugged into the financial side of the property with him to make sure he's managing it properly. He has learned the essentials as I've assisted him in setting it up to stay out of trouble.

On a more general side of guiding, my next son started college this fall. He also started his first job away from home this past summer. He's also on the varsity cross country team at college. So during the summer he was working and training with the cross country team. It was a very busy summer for him. He works at a restaurant, and they knew he'd be going to school so his schedule would have to be changed once classes started. They did alter the schedule around his classes, but I noticed that he was still working some fairly long hours during the week. I sat down with him to map out all of his duties between class, study, running, and work. We quickly saw he had very little time for study and assignments outside of class. I advised him that he should tell his employer that he could only work weekends while classes were taking place, and they made that change. This is the type of guidance and involvement we need to have with our older kids. They may not know that they are overloaded until it's way too late and a lower-priority activity has suffered. We can help with a bird's-eye view of things in alerting them before they make significant mistakes.

Quality Social Outlets

The most important thing for young adults aside for their values is going to be their social involvements. It's an age that's a bit carefree where the responsibilities of a family don't have them tied down yet. I encourage my children at this stage to enjoy their involvements and recreational time. It doesn't have to be constant or perpetual. Some will get their fill of it before others, but it is good to have that opportunity instead of young people forcing themselves into commitments because of making mistakes.

They will want to meet new people and make new friends and acquaintances. This is a very healthy thing for them to do. As fathers we can guide them in making decisions of where to plug themselves in socially. They have to remember that as Catholics they are not going to fit into every social circle. If they try to, then they will end up lowering their standards and likely falling into more serious sin. It is important that they know they type of company they can be around without being unduly influenced. They also need to be reminded that they are to maintain their standards for themselves and to assist and influence others to uphold or raise their standards.

This stage is where their self-image becomes so important. They need to feel that it is not only OK, but best for them to just be themselves. When anyone tries to put up a façade that they are something they are not, it is only a cause for trouble. This often causes young people great difficulty as they try to find themselves and try to fit in to social circles. They may express a desire to "fit in," but we'll have to remind them that if they have to change for others, they are not being genuine. Of course this is not to say that they shouldn't try to overcome their faults which may cause others to resist them. Here we're talking about them keeping higher standards not relaxing standards and wondering why they aren't accepted by those who possess higher standards. They have to learn to form habits of being considerate of others and not being self-centered. This is building toward them learning to acquire quality, valuable unselfish relationships and eventually culminating in relationships that become permanent whether in marriage or religious communities.

Most of our children will eventually marry. They have to have social outlets where they will be able to find a spouse. We have to ensure that these quality outlets are available to them so they do not feel hopeless and consider accepting a relationship lesser than that of their calling. We have to remain accessible to them as they go through this process of forming more mature relationships and work through the difficulties they encounter with them. We continue to guide them with the wisdom of our age and experience.

The Good Life

It is quite rewarding to work years and years in rearing and training children then seeing them plug themselves into a place in society where they are welcomed because of the value they bring. When you encounter people and they tell you how much they enjoy and benefit from having your children around, you know that you're hard work has paid off. This is the goal in raising our sons and daughters, to raise adults, not children.

Contrast that with some parents who are living through what seems like hell because their children have tragic problems after having made disastrous choices. On the other extreme, the goal is not to shelter them perpetually and do everything for them never allowing them to reach full adulthood. I've seen this happen in families as well. So often many families with successful businesses or wealth will just pass everything on to their children without ever teaching them how they acquired it. It should be with great caution that a parent works a child into their family business. The morale issues that surround this in the workplace can sometimes be insurmountable. Ideally the kids would go off and work to learn the skill that may be used in the family business in a workplace that is separate from the family where they will be handled and judged objectively. Then once the necessary skills are acquired and the experience has been gained, they can be hired on in the family business.

We can see that all situations have their challenges. The grass isn't always greener on the other side of the fence. Keeping the goal in focus of instilling in each of our children the dignity of becoming and independent member of society will assist us in guiding them along their way. This is where we stand now with our family as our children start to really make their way and prove value in the world. It is very rewarding. This is why this book has been written. I often ask someone to see the skins on the wall that they've acquired or accomplished before following their advice. We have adult children and younger children, all still within the Catholic Church and striving to live in a state of Grace. A parent couldn't ask much more than that. We've seen the principles outlined in this book produce these results for others. We've followed them, and we have had them produce the same for us.

CHAPTER 15

Your Mission

Finally, draw your strength from the Lord and from his mighty power. Put on the armor of God so that you may be able to stand firm against the tactics of the devil.(Eph 6:10-11)

We don't become men of by accident but by a very deliberate decision followed up with commitment toward its accomplishment.

Congratulations, you've reached the final chapter of this book. You hold in your hands the handbook to Catholic manhood today. Use it as a reference as you go through the progression from one stage to the next. This book has been laid out for you to be your guide, one you can return to again and again. As you come to experience each stage of growth in manhood, you will come to recognize and understand these stages better and will better be able to anticipate the next. All the while the virtues taught will equip and enable you through each stage.

Your Mission, If You Choose to Accept It

Just as though you were working each part of your body as a bodybuilder, work each part of your character as outlined in Part I in building your true inner manhood, regardless of your present stage. These are strengths that we naturally possess as men. We need to glory in these powerful gifts with which God has blessed us. We all will have them in varying degrees. As some men will have more upper body strength than lower, some of us will be stronger in some virtues as opposed to others. We need them all to be the man God has called us to be.

We should never shrink from our masculine gifts and traits or hide them as though they may be something to be ashamed of or things that should be "toned down" or inhibited. We need to live our masculinity out loud. God created us this way for a reason: because the world and society needs real unabashed truly masculine men who are strong and solid, yet disciplined and controlled. True manhood is a responsible use of some very powerful traits for the good of others. Just as soldiers in the military use the power of their force for the national defense, so the man in society and in the home does the same in a non-violent and domestic sense. It is for the good of others that manhood plays itself out, not for self-indulgence.

The hope of the author of this book is that the reader will find order in the framework that has been outlined here, not to create an overwhelming burden. Often when we are faced with a task, there is some uncertainty of how it will play out. Do I have everything I need? What if this happens or that happens? By laying out this framework, we take a lot of the unknown out of the equation so that it can be solved. Often we have to reduce things to writing and organize them all in one place so they are not scattered are confused. Striving for the developing manhood will be complex, but it does not have to be complicated. When approached and attempted with no order it will be complicated. With order and discipline, it is an adventure beyond compare.

The Battle

Men are built for combat; we are battle ready. Make no mistake, life is a battle. Even if you are not an actual military soldier, you were built for combat. Ever since the powers of darkness were embraced by Lucifer and he fell from the heavens at the hands of St. Michael, the battle between good and evil has been raging. Every man born into the world is called to fight this battle. We fight it as men, in a masculine fashion. This doesn't mean that we are required to be violent, but it also doesn't mean that we are lead by prevailing emotion.

The Church has equipped us with so many ways to fortify our masculinity in body and soul. Prayer, fast, abstinence, and almsgiving are all ways that reign in our manhood and channel it to produce greater power. It is like a powerful river. When water is dispersed around raining and in puddles, it is somewhat mild. But when it is channeled by the banks of a river, it can produce great power. It is the same with the disciplines given to us by the Church.

Always remember our Blessed Mother who is there for us to provide the closest intercession to her Son. She is a guide for us on the way. She is an ally who will stand by us fearlessly and fight with us. This is the role given to Her by our Heavenly Father. She loves us dearly like a Mother and only wants what is best for us. Do not disappoint your Mother.

Conclusion

Catholic Manhood Today. Catholic-Manhood-Today. We live in times that are a bit complex. It's been better, and it's been worse. If there was ever a time when real Catholic men were needed, today would be one of those times. We are blessed. We have the

Church with her treasury of Graces from the Sacraments and timeless teachings to guide us on the way. What has been shared in this book is all based on those teachings applied in contemporary society. "And God created man to his own image: to the image of God he created him: male and female he created them."(Gen 1:27) He did not create us to be women or to be like women. We need to live out our masculinity completely without compromise using our strength and gifts for the protection of others and for the good of society. If we do we will experience true fulfillment and give glory to God.